The Best Thing That Could Ever Happen to You:

How a Career Reversal

Can Reinvigorate

Your Life

Sander A. Flaum

with Mechele Flaum

The Best Thing That Could Ever Happen to You: How a Career Reversal Can Reinvigorate Your Life

© 2013 Sander A. Flaum

ISBN

987-0-98-905130-9 print edition

987-0-98-905131-6 e-book edition

Published by Big Shoes Publishing

Cover design by Mallory Rock

Cartoon by Mike Shapiro, page 116, used by permission

Contents

Acknowledgments

First, hats off to my brilliant collaborator, John McCarty. John never missed a deadline, was a great interviewer, and, most of all, was a brilliant listener—the sign of a great leader. And thank you, wise Madeleine Morel, for introducing me to John.

We interviewed some of the best executive recruiters in the country for their insights on what works for unemployed candidates and, more importantly, what doesn't work. John Archer, Bob Atkins, Denise DeMan, and Nomi Edwards (Director of Human Resources, Philosophy IB) were our brainpower in this endeavor. What would this book be without them?

Kudos and thanks also to Alison Simard, our creative and talented PR person, who helped with the book's branding; to our terrific webmaster, Michael Welch; and to Ellen Leviss for her Human Resources counsel.

Hats off as well to Amy Edelman at IndieReader Publishing Services and her extraordinary crew, notably our talented and capable editor Grace Spampinato and designer Edward Charlton at Scribbulations, for helping us with the finishing touches to convey the book's important message. Amy gave us her savvy wisdom on a publishing strategy for the book, along with public relations and distribution planning, and her internal team made every word count in look and meaning. This team was awesome.

Thanks and love to my bright and beautiful daughter, Pamela, whose expertise in personal branding helped me greatly. And hugs to my dear cousin, Dr. Stanley Kissel, my go-to guy and my inspiration.

Finally, a big bow to my loyal executive assistant for more than ten years, Lisa Pollione, for her diligence and patience (most of the time anyway) in putting the manuscript together for me in a timely fashion.

I have saved the best for last—my wonderful wife and best friend Mechele. She challenged me on style and content, edited my text, and imbedded all the confidence in me I needed to complete the book. She is the best thing that ever happened to me.

Sander A. Flaum

Foreword

It's All About Moving Ahead

Never in my wildest dreams as a boy growing up in small-town New Concord, Ohio, in the 1930s could I ever have imagined the then unforeseen events—and great opportunities—that would shape my life: World War II, the Korean War, test-flying new military aircraft, flying two flights into space, US Senator for twenty-four years, and now to be part of the John Glenn School of Public Affairs at the Ohio State University.

Not long ago, my wife Annie remarked, "We've had a great life." I corrected her to change the tense to "are having a great life." I believe that tense change reflects how we look at the future no matter our actual age.

But all of us have good things—and not so good things—happen at each stage of our lives and that is what Sander's book is about. How do we deal with those "not so good" events that could overwhelm or, in turn, be overcome? I've had ups and downs like everyone else. Let me give you just one example.

A couple of years after our first orbital space flight, I was leaving NASA and had announced my candidacy for the United States Senate. A home accident left me in no condition to continue the campaign, since the doctors predicted it would be probably the better part of a year before I would be fully operational again. So I withdrew from the campaign and spent the better part of that year fortunately getting a full recovery, but it was a miserable year.

In the next election for the Senate, I once again declared my candidacy and campaigned very hard but lost in the primary. That was a bitter pill. In effect, I kept on campaigning and four years later was elected overwhelmingly to the Senate where I spent the next twenty-four years.

The point here, as Sander writes, is that, in life, you must keep moving forward with passion and persistence to advance past the setbacks and disappointments you inevitably encounter. My friend Sander's take is that, when one chapter of your life ends, it's time to start re-energizing yourself and write the next.

I've known Sander for close to twenty-five years, and I know that, like us all, he's seen his own ups and downs. But he's the writer, so I'll let him explain. Enjoy *The Best Thing That Could Ever Happen to You*!

John Glenn

Introduction

The Best Thing...REALLY!

Let me tell you about Jack. He's a tall, good-looking dude, smart as a whip, and a nice guy in the bargain. He worked as a copywriter for a mid-level advertising firm catering to the financial services sector in San Francisco. Jack's skills as a wordsmith, capable of turning the driest products and services into the most tantalizing must-haves, captured the attention of an affiliate agency across the country in New York City. Sensing potential managerial material in Jack's creativity and job performance, the New York affiliate offered him a job managing the agency's creative department.

Taking the position meant relocating lock, stock, and barrel 3,000 miles away to New York—a big move. Jack talked it over with his wife, and together, they decided it was too good an opportunity for Jack to pass up, especially since his eye had been on moving up the corporate ladder anyway, and there were no such opportunities at his present firm. So Jack said yes.

After a period spent finding an apartment in Brooklyn and settling into his new life in the city, Jack seized the reigns of his new managerial position with the kind of gusto employers like. But over time, his bosses, including the agency's CEO, began hearing comments from clients about certain "difficulties" they were having working with Jack. Inquiring into the matter quietly, they learned that Jack was not a great communicator or collaborator; in fact, he projected an attitude almost of condescension—that, from a creative standpoint, he always knew best. To some of his clients and coworkers, his attitude bordered on arrogance.

There was no doubt that Jack had a terrifically creative mind, but he appeared to lack the skill, or even aptitude, for building relationships with people on a professional level—a skill critical to managerial success in any business or institution.

After about a year, during which the negative feedback about Jack only increased, his supervisors realized they had made a definite mistake putting him in a managerial position. But knowing he had uprooted himself and his family (which now included a first child) to accept the job, they offered him a position as senior copywriter in the company's sister agency. Seeing this as a personal rebuff and a comedown from his management spot, Jack refused and his employers asked him to resign, which he did with stoic professionalism—all the while seething inside.

Jack fumed for days that stretched into weeks. He was happy living in New York and didn't want to uproot his family again. Nor did he want to go back to being just a copywriter. His anger and frustration over losing his job soon developed into feelings of self-doubt—maybe he didn't have what it takes to be a good leader and a success in life.

These feelings of unworthiness began to creep over into his behavior. On some days, he didn't bother to shave; on others, he didn't bother to get dressed. "How can I get even with those bastards for what they've done to me?" he pondered. His mind was awhirl, going in every direction at once and taking him nowhere. He needed work but was getting little or no response to his applications, not even requests for an exploratory interview. Had his former supervisors been right? "What in hell is going on here?" he asked himself day after day—until one day, he began to answer his own question.

His former employer hadn't hired him just for fun! The company had seen something in him. Perhaps all those years of working alone, inside his own head, at his Mac keyboard had shut him off from understanding the other basic requirements of functioning successfully in the business world. As smart and as articulate as he was, with a great creative mind, Jack now was getting the idea that unless he could manage to combine those important strengths with the ability to relate to coworkers and clients on a personal level, he would always be just a follower, never the big idea leader he wanted to be. That moment was the turning point for Jack.

Understanding this enabled him not only to see his own strengths clearly again but also to realize that he could improve upon them. Like any already-good product or service that can be improved, Jack could build himself into a better version, one that could be repackaged and relaunched into the marketplace with a much more successful result.

In an effort to rebrand himself, Jack talked to colleagues and friends, and even some former clients in San Francisco and in New York, seeking their unfettered views of him and building a solid network of confidants and contacts along the way. He took a course at Fordham Graduate School of Business Administration on building interpersonal relationship skills. He then accepted a mid-level executive position at a small advertising shop that required him to draw upon all of his skills new and old. He worked hard and racked up some big early wins using his newly learned skills and, to no one's surprise, was subsequently recruited by a larger agency, where eventually he became CEO.

Jack is now the president of a major global advertising network. He is also the board chair for a noted nonprofit institution, which he runs not only to broaden himself but, more importantly, to give back. Now Jack looks upon that resignation as the best thing that could have ever happened to him.

Unemployment Today a Universal Problem

Everyone who has ever been let go in a corporate downsizing, been fired from a leadership or any other position of responsibility, lost a promised promotion, or languished in a dead-end job due to temporary inertia or fear—of losing benefits or income—can empathize with some aspect of Jack's story. At some point in our working lives, most of us, like Jack, have found ourselves riding a similar roller coaster as we struggled to regain our self-worth and win employment again after a devastating professional setback. In other words, we've all been there. Millions are there now.

According to US Department of Labor statistics, millions of Americans are officially out of work every day. And millions more out-of-work Americans fall off the department's rolls of the unemployed, having exhausted their unemployment insurance benefits.

Other statistics from Pew Research show that more than one in four Americans who are gainfully employed hate their job for one reason or another. But they stay in place, unhappy and unproductive, because they believe their prospects for better employment are poor in a dismal job market. They stay—until they get downsized or outright fired.

Adding to the problem, the government is so mired in debt and political squabbling that it is unable, unwilling, or both to come up with any significant jobs programs comparable to those of the 1930s. Those programs put millions of unemployed Americans back to productive work rebuilding the country's infrastructure— as teachers, plumbers, electricians, firefighters, and so forth— providing a jolt to the economy and bringing it back to life.

Yes, it's a mess out there and many people no longer believe in the system or feel hope, having lost faith in their political and corporate leaders to straighten the mess out. Worst of all, many lose faith in themselves to control their own destiny.

The Best Thing That Could Ever Happen to You speaks to this lack of hope and loss of faith head-on. In a realistic and practical way, I want to provide those of you who are out of work or unhappy and unfulfilled in your jobs the ability to recognize what you personally can control and to empower you to create the next, fulfilling chapter in your working life. You don't have to be running unhappily in place on a treadmill going nowhere.

My Goal

In challenging times like these, you've got to move forward in a positive mode, just as Jack finally did. Fear, uncertainty, and self-doubt are the enemy. Your weapons to fight the enemy are inner strength, confidence, courage, persistency, and resiliency. Hitting back accomplishes nothing. Retreating into depression leads nowhere.

And so, the purpose of this book is to share what's worked for my junior and senior colleagues and friends who have bounced back, stronger than ever, from a career reversal: a set of best practices, strategies, tips, and proven techniques that you can use to reinvigorate your own working life and that are fine-tuned to the needs of today's job seekers at every level, whether unemployed or underemployed.

My goal for this book is to provide you with a concise, easy to understand, and foolproof process to identify the myths and the core issues (saboteurs) that stand in your way of success on the job front and to enable you to work through them. It is a process designed for anyone in turmoil—from being frustrated in his or her job, from being thrown suddenly out of work, or from being unemployed for a long period—who does not know what to do or where to turn.

My method grew out of my background as marketing head of a major pharmaceutical company and then as CEO of a global advertising and consulting company, where I counseled scores of colleagues, clients, and my MBA students at Fordham University. I've done this work with senior level executives (CEOs and company presidents), middle management executives, entrepreneurs, sales professionals, newly minted MBAs, and even politicians. Serving as an Adjunct Professor of Management Systems and Executive-in-Residence, I teach at the Fordham University Graduate School of Business Administration. I'm also founder and chair of its Leadership Forum—where, among other aspects of business management, I also teach leadership skills to MBAs. In my many years of consulting and mentoring, I have identified common threads in behavior among those who have suffered career setbacks by examining how they coped with those setbacks, how they rebounded from them, and how they turned a loss into a gain, creating an opportunity to rejuvenate their professional and personal lives.

Because I went through a major professional setback in my own life, I was able to see how these same threads ran through my own experience. Like these other professionals, I went into an emotional tailspin fueled by unhealthy, unproductive feelings that I gradually—and with difficulty—pulled myself out of, regaining a sense of clarity and purpose.

Focusing at last on my strengths and not on the feeling that the whole world was out to get me, I was able, like Jack, to turn a corner in my own professional life, eventually becoming chairman of Euro RSCG Life (now Havas Life), a large global healthcare communications network. After fifteen years at the helm, I left to create my own consulting company, Flaum Navigators, using skills

I had never lost, but had come to undervalue, plus newly acquired ones in twenty-first century marketing, sales effectiveness, and leadership. I learned from some wonderful mentors that Innovation + Leadership = Growth. This formula is the underpinning of what I call the "Big Idea" principle. And to help marketing and sales teams think and execute in new ways, I have created a "Big Idea" model that generates compelling strategies and tactics to jump the revenue curve.

Maybe everyone can't run a business, but everyone can use this book's well-researched best practices to rejuvenate and enrich their individual careers at whatever level they choose—even in a tight job market. The effort needed to rebound from a job loss can be likened to waging a war, and the effects of prolonged unemployment can result in a kind of battle fatigue. The diverse but related threads in my professional life have enabled me to construct a method to combat battle fatigue and turn it into a battle plan that will work for anybody.

How to Use This Book

When people lose their jobs or find themselves stuck in a dead-end job they hate but can't afford to leave, the experience often triggers several conflicting but uniformly negative emotions. If not dealt with immediately and overcome, or at least held in check, these emotions lead to obsessing so much over the problem (the job or career reversal) that all focus on a solution to that problem is lost, making a bad situation worse.

The Best Thing That Could Ever Happen to You addresses this dilemma by giving you a weapon to face down these counterproductive demons and combat them. I call these demons "The Four Stages of Sabotaging Yourself":

Stage 1: Anger

Stage 2: Recrimination

Stage 3: Depression

Stage 4: Unfocused and Unproductive Behavior

You will learn how to fight off these negative emotions and frustrations with persistence, passion, and deliberate practice to get yourself back on track. You will see how to convert

1. Anger to Positive Action

2. Recrimination to Outshining Your Rejecters

3. Depression to Motivation

4. Unfocused and Unproductive Behavior to Clarity and Purpose

leading to...Success!

You will learn how to channel the negative emotions, following a job loss or some other professional setback, into a constructive, motivational driver that unleashes your inner man or woman of steel. Thus enabled, you can create a rich environment of professional opportunity.

Jobs are always available for the taking. If you've worked successfully in new business development, sales, project management or created exceptional value in your professional space, you WILL get a job. If you think you haven't the skill set, look at your career to date and think again. It's all about attitude—making a commitment to work harder and think smarter than your competitors—and about energy—taking a leadership role in your own life. By following this formula, the unmarketable or unemployable you will increase the chances of again becoming marketable and employable, fueled by the certain knowledge that *Yes, I can do this and be successful at it!*

The process is twofold:

In Part I, you will come to a deeper understanding of what's been happening to you on an emotional and behavioral level after an employment setback. You will be able to identify issues—cultural myths you may have bought into—that may actually be working against your prospects of reentering the workforce. When you confront the counterproductive emotions and behaviors stemming from these myths, you will exponentially increase your chances of besting the competition and getting the job or promotion you want.

Part I is where you will

- delve deeply into the issues (attitudes, external causes, internal fears, or a combination of each) underlying what's holding you back from finding and getting the new job or promotion you're looking for,

- release your self-inflicted blockage by bringing negative emotions to the surface and clearing them away to create a new path of opportunity,

- determine who YOU are by utilizing an exercise that identifies the reasons why you're valuable to yourself and to an employer.

In Part II, you will combine your newfound focus with some straightforward strategies, tools, tips, and techniques to

- develop your personal brand, so you can uniquely position and brand yourself vis-à-vis your competitors,

- successfully crack open the job market,

- secure better, more lucrative, more fulfilling employment elsewhere,

- land that sought-after position.

Once you have landed that promotion, new job, or desired position, you will learn about creating the 100 Day Plan to successfully secure your situation. This strategy is readily adaptable to anyone's level of experience and need.

A TOTAL Solution

I know there are at least a gazillion formulas out there for job seeking in a so-called "jobless" economy. And they all focus on the same advice: how to assemble a résumé that puts your best foot forward, how to dress for success at that all-important interview, and so on. It isn't that these instructions don't play a role in securing gainful employment, it's that they put the cart before the horse.

Without systematic exercises to develop and project a positive attitude, without reviving the skills you may have forgotten you possess, without sufficiently contemplating the job or career direction you want to go in and what it is YOU want in terms of job satisfaction—in other words, without proper focus up front—the most eye-catching outfit or the most impressive résumé in the world won't you get you where you want to go.

The Best Thing That Could Ever Happen to You goes beyond the traditional formulas for employment success. It gets to the root of what's really holding you back from rebounding successfully after a tough professional setback and shows you how to use that setback as an opportunity to recharge your life, turn the page, and create a brilliant new chapter if you desire.

If you can't identify fairly rapidly what's in your way and combine that knowledge with a way to achieve positive change, your percentage of success is dramatically reduced. So your new mantra and goal is to achieve the outcome you seek—being employed at a job you enjoy—in less time.

The Best Thing That Could Ever Happen to You is packed with anecdotes, self-exercises, and checklists drawn from my workshops and coaching sessions, as well as from personal stories of my own and my clients' battles with career reversal. It also includes "Recruiter Memos"—special insider tips and Do's and Don'ts direct from the mouths of some of the smartest recruiters in the employment business. Many of these nuggets of advice have never been shared before and will help guide you in avoiding all the pitfalls to getting the position you want.

This book will show you how to

- understand, manage, and be free of your inhibitors to get the new job,

- focus on your present or prospective employer's true wants and expand your professional skills to increase job options, recognition, and rewards,

- translate your self-worth into a compelling brand and develop a plan to sell it. Your brand will reflect who you are—a person with self-assurance and authority who, most importantly, demonstrates what you can do for your employer,

- reinvigorate your working and personal life by being more satisfied and enthusiastic on the job,

- improve your mental health and happiness through pride of accomplishment and bolstered self-esteem.

In short, if you are unemployed or unsatisfied at work and looking for a way back to a productive life, *The Best Thing That Could Ever Happen to You* is the best book that could ever happen to you.

Part I

"YOU'RE FIRED!"

Chapter 1

You Are What You Think

"Myths which are believed in tend to become true."
-- George Orwell (1903-1950), Author

You've known them—maybe now you're even among them—the walking wounded, for whom taking on the job market is a monumental trial. A trial similar to the Greek myth of King Sisyphus, who constantly pushed a huge boulder up a hill without ever reaching the top. He remained in that no-win, painful position forever, pushing forward and falling back, forward and back, getting nowhere fast—and with no benefits or time off either!

If you have ever felt like King Sisyphus or are feeling like him now because you were let go from a job, lost out on a big promotion, or are suffering in silence at a job you hate for fear of trying to better yourself in a tight job market, a combination of factors are probably holding you back from reaching the top of that hill. And a tight job market is the least of those factors.

This first chapter focuses on the widespread and most common beliefs people share about job hunting, the job market, and their employability in that market—beliefs that often prevent you from securing gainful, fulfilling employment or, perhaps, even looking for it. These beliefs—I call them the "ten biggest myths"—affect our attitudes and the way we think about our employability. I'm exposing them here because they often erode our confidence while we try to find work or a better, more rewarding position.

These myths and misconceptions, which you may even be buying into right now, are

1. "It's the end of the world!"
2. "It's all their fault!"
3. "It's my fault!"
4. "If I failed once, I'll probably fail again."
5. "What I have to offer obviously is not that important."
6. "I'm doing everything I can. There are just no jobs out there for me."
7. "I have to be perfect and I can't be."
8. "Change is too frightening for me to handle!"
9. "Finding something new is too daunting and overwhelming a task."
10. "I'm too chunky, too short, too awkward, too talkative, or inarticulate."

Let's look at each one and separate the facts from the fiction.

Myth #1: "It's the end of the world!"

Steve, fifty-five, was a print salesman in Kenosha, Wisconsin. He'd been selling business cards, letterheads, brochures, and a host of other printing services to numerous companies and retailers all over southern Wisconsin for about twenty years. Then came Staples, along with desktop publishing, Photoshop, and other technology changes that have enabled businesses to handle most kinds of print jobs in-house. And Steve's position was eliminated.

The company that had employed him was still in business, but it retained only its top sales reps after downsizing. Steve wasn't considered to be in that lofty category; he was a slightly above-average performer. But when the bottom fell out of the printing services market, any kind of average was no longer good enough to keep him employed and make a decent living. So when he got the news that he was being downsized, Steve went into shock. "Oh my God," he said, "I'm fifty-five years old! What'll I do now? Print services are tanking. Who'll give me a job? How will I support my family and keep my daughter in college?"

Eighteen frustrating months later, depressed and still looking for work in print sales, he was bemoaning the "fact" that it was the "end of the world." He was convinced it had come. But I am here to tell you: It's a myth!

A terrible tragedy such as the sudden death of a child, parent, spouse, or other loved one can be the end of the world. But losing a job because your company was sold off or downsized, as in Steve's case? No. That's not the end of the world—unless you let it be. On the contrary, it's an open door not a closed one. It opens up new possibilities, but only if you let it.

Steve was finally convinced by his family and some former business associates to try his hand at something other than selling, which, he even admitted to himself, was something he'd never excelled at nor particularly liked. What he did enjoy about the job of selling was the social aspect—meeting new people and trying to help them. What he didn't like was the selling part and having to hit sales quotas.

From a friend's daughter, who worked as an ER physician at an area hospital, Steve learned of a job opening in Admissions. The salary wasn't as good as what he'd been earning in sales, but the job description appealed to him: interacting with many different kinds of people, some in distress, and trying to help them without having to sell them anything. So he went after the job, got it, and now, almost a year later, he's happier than the proverbial clam. Not just because he's gainfully employed again but also because he's proven himself to be extremely good at the job. He enjoys it, and his boss appreciates his efforts!

My point is that the world does not end, even though it may feel like it does at the time, and one can recover from losing a job or missing out on an important promotion. There is always another opportunity waiting in the wings, provided you are willing to open yourself up to the possibility, to move on, to embrace change, and to start focusing on the next chapter of your life. Maybe the pay won't be as good. Or maybe it will turn out to be even better. Who knows?

The key to job security is to find something you like, as Steve finally did. Because those who excel are those who truly enjoy what they do, and they are seldom let go, except under the most extreme circumstances (such as operations shifting to Bangladesh and key employees not wanting to uproot themselves or their families). Lee Iacocca, former chairman of the Chrysler Corporation, affirms the importance of liking your job: "What is it that you like doing? If you don't like it, get out of it, because you'll be lousy at it. You don't have to stay with a job for the rest of your life, because if you don't like it you'll never be successful in it."

Falling victim to a belief that the world has ended is just an exercise in self-pity. Clear heads don't buy into that belief—certainly not for long anyway. Clear heads take the lead in their own working lives, as you must, if you want to dispel rather than keep wallowing in this myth.

Myth #2: "It's all their fault!"

When we lose our jobs or languish in ones we've come to hate because we aren't moving up (or even sideways), our inclination is always to blame the owner, the boss, our manager—but not ourselves. "It's all their fault I'm in this position," we say. "My boss is an idiot." Or "She likes the guy in the next cubicle a lot more than me."

Far be it for me to suggest that there aren't any idiots or racists in management positions. There are, and plenty of them too. But even so, it's never all their fault if you find yourself on the chopping block, consistently not promoted, or just plain bored out of your skull doing what you're doing. That's a myth—and dangerous to persist in believing it.

If you are doing an A or A-Plus job and have received a steady stream of performance reviews indicating this or stating that you have fully overcome any previous performance deficiencies, then clearly you won't be let go or passed over. Even managers who are idiots and racists are not dumb enough to let an A performer go, not even in a downsizing.

I recently consulted with a major corporation in the process of downsizing 10,000 of its employees. That's a lot of people, more than the population of many cities. But I guarantee you (and not because I've got any insider information either) that not one of those 10,000 is an A performer. Most companies and institutions hold onto and reward A and A-Plus performers at all costs.

Whether you're in research, operations, marketing, sales, information technology (IT), or whatever, if you can be counted on to help keep the organization jumping the innovation, productivity, or revenue curve, you will keep your job, no matter how much belt-tightening is undertaken. The C performers go first and, if necessary, then the B performers. Seldom, if ever, are those who contribute extraordinary value let go.

Of course, one may say that in situations where employers let people go because of a move to another state or overseas, it is their fault you're out of a job. But you haven't been singled out; everybody else who worked this job is now unemployed as well, perhaps even some A performers who declined to relocate. But, even under that circumstance, laying blame gets you nowhere. It's a pointless exercise. You must quickly get past fixing the blame on them. You must get over it and move on.

Myth #3: "It's my fault!"

I'll share more stories in subsequent chapters, but this one incident about myself exposes the insidiousness of this myth particularly well, so I'll share it with you now. Back in the early 1980s while working in the pharmaceutical industry, I was recruited by a competitor. I wasn't dissatisfied with my job, but I was ambitious and had my eye on a senior management position.

The competitor's offer was for the job of Chief Marketing Officer. Hearing of this, my employer made me an offer I couldn't refuse: it matched the competitor's offer financially and promised me the C-Suite job the following year. So I stayed on happily where I was. But when the time finally came to fill that spot, I was unexpectedly passed over, and the job was given to someone else.

I was devastated by this turn of events, of course, and felt betrayed. I knew I couldn't continue to stay at the company under those circumstances, so I jumped ship and took another job at a top-ranked advertising agency where I was promised the president's position, which would open up when the current president retired. But that didn't pan out either. Business got so good under my stewardship that he decided not to retire after all. Yet another promise unkept! But I digress. Let's go back to my first brush with corporate betrayal.

In addition to feeling devastated, I also harbored the suspicion that it was my fault I'd been passed over because of a handicap

I've worked hard all my life to overcome. I'm a stutterer and have been since I was a kid. Through a lot of effort over the years to control it, my stuttering is less pronounced now, but it is still there—and I was convinced it had cost me the top spot.

After I left the pharmaceutical company in 1982, I subsequently learned from a former member of the board of directors that one of the other board members had vetoed my elevation because of his ignorant belief that stuttering was a form of mental illness! I don't know why it never occurred to him to speculate on why "mental illness" had not kept me from generating more revenue for the company than anybody else. Here I had been blaming myself when it was ignorance, even prejudice, on the part of one member of the board that had torpedoed me. The company had made a mistake, which it fully acknowledged after the person they had selected fell below expectations. That's when they called and offered me the Chief Marketing Officer position with a huge pay increase. But by then I had successfully moved on and declined their offer with pleasure.

The point of my story is that I had bought into the myth that it was my fault I had been passed over. It wasn't true. I wasn't to blame any more than one board member's ignorance about my speech disorder. The board's giving me a thumbs-down was the fault of every other board member, or even the company itself. I'd fallen into playing the blame game and it was that which, however briefly, had prevented me from being able to move ahead with clarity and purpose to do even better.

But, it IS your fault if you do something stupid that gets you passed over, demoted, or fired. In that case, own up to it fast so you can move on.

For example, a neighbor of mine who worked in the electronics business once told me about something stupid he did. His boss, the Sales VP, told him it looked like the company was not going to make its quarter, which meant the board wouldn't be very happy and they'd kill any bonuses. So he urged my neighbor to overstock his wholesalers. They wouldn't have to pay for the overstocked orders until the products were actually sold in the following quarters, but the volume increase in orders would look good on the books. My friend shouldn't have succumbed to the pressure tactics and should've rejected his boss's advice. But he didn't, which he now deeply regrets, and the industry oversight folks caught the ploy. He was not let go immediately, but soon after; so were the Finance and Sales VPs and the CEO. They had all done a stupid thing.

In such a situation, you've got to take the hit, face up to your shortcomings, listen to good advice and get in charge of your life again, and move on. If you just keep beating yourself up about being gutless, you'll only wind up in a downward spiral, chasing your own tail. Better to man up and learn from your mistakes and move forward.

Myth #4: "If I failed once, I'll probably fail again."

If this one were true, humankind would never have landed on the moon, or had an electric light, or achieved anything else for that matter. We'd still be in the Stone Age, living in caves and throwing rocks at each other.

The more you keep believing this myth, the more you'll cling to it, and the more self-fulfilling the prophecy of failing becomes. "I'll never have as good a job, as expensive a car, or as nice a house as the guy up the street. I guess I'm just a loser." I hear this a lot in my mentoring work, and I have come to recognize the sentiment for what it really is—an expression of self-pity, or depression, but also a clear sign of low self-esteem.

If these refrains get frequent enough where they keep you from even getting off the couch to find a job, then it's time to get some help (see Chapters 2 and 3).

If you'll recall my earlier story in Myth #1 about Steve the print salesman, he had come to believe he was a loser too. He had been an average salesman in every sales job he'd ever had. As a result, failing in sales—at earning bonuses, getting promotions, or finally just holding on to his job—had become a way of life for him. And why? Not because he really was a loser, but because a critical part of selling—building relationships to make the numbers—was just not his thing. Once he recognized this, he no longer believed that he was condemned to keep failing at every possible job because he had failed at selling.

There are always other issues at play. Like Steve, you too could be in the wrong job or the wrong business. Now Steve is doing work that he fully enjoys and can excel at, and so he's not failing! You can excel too because there is absolutely no truth to the idea that just because you failed once, you have to fail again.

Myth #5: "What I have to offer is obviously not that important."

If you have been told in performance reviews that you need to show improvement in areas X, Y, and Z in order to meet expectations, and you are subsequently demoted, laid off, or dismissed for not doing so, it's not because what you have to offer is unimportant, it's that what you have to offer in observed value is insufficient. You haven't demonstrated a willingness, a determination, or even an eagerness to improve, let alone go the extra mile to excel. You're viewed as just average.

And as I've said, the ordinary are the ones let go or passed over every year, particularly by large-scale employers. While job performance may be good enough to warrant a paycheck in good times, when performance falls well short of others in the group or the industry standard, an employer has no reason to keep average performers in challenging times.

If what you are offering today isn't sufficient to lift the perception of you out of the ranks of "average" in what you do or how you do it, ultimately the likelihood is you will wind up in the unemployment line. It's up to you. Do you want to remain "ordinary" and vulnerable to losing your job or being stuck in a low-paying, dead-end one? Or do you want to be the go-to person with the Big Ideas, a top performer at whatever job you hold?

A lot of people are just content to be average. But it's not a given that they have to be. So if you feel that what you have to offer is not considered important, then maybe it's time to start offering something that is. Nobody wants a legacy that reads "average" or "ordinary."

Myth #6: "I'm doing everything I can. There are just no jobs out there for me."

Let's take a look at the first half of this two-part myth.

You've lost your job, or want a better one. So what are you doing to find one? When I ask this of most people, they typically say, "Well, I go through the online job boards every day. I go on Craigslist.com and Monster.com and twenty other websites to look for opportunities in my field. What else can I do?" My typical reply is, "Obviously, that's not enough, let alone all you can do." Nor may those things even be the right ones to do in your particular situation.

Here's why. You're just going through the motions, which is why your efforts are not getting results. You are looking for the position where you think you will fit best rather than looking for the position that might best fit you and your future. The latter is what gives you the leg up on any competition you may have for a job; it shows a strong commitment to excel that tends to result in employment—a clear win-win situation for you and the employer combined. So, if what you are doing is not working, then you are not doing what you actually need to do. I'll go into this in more detail in the upcoming chapters of this book.

Now for the second part of this myth—that there are no jobs out there for you. Wrong! There are plenty of jobs available. A multitude of them, in fact. There may be just no jobs where you're looking.

Consider Salesman Steve again. At more than one point during his eighteen months of looking for a print sales position and not finding one, he threw up his hands in desperation, feeling that there were just no jobs out there for him. In one sense he was right—there were no jobs out there for him in print sales, a disappearing business in which he'd been an average performer. But as we've seen, it turned out there was a job for him, wasn't there? One that fit him like a glove, but in a field—hospital admissions—he had never considered before. Up to then, he'd been going about finding employment all wrong because he'd been continually looking in all the wrong places.

I'll share a little employment secret with you here that recruiters have shared with me. If you keep running into a brick wall with your résumé and getting no requests for an interview, then you haven't got the goods the employer is looking for, or your former employer is not being terribly flattering, or your résumé isn't selling you correctly. Likewise, if you are told that your background and experience look good but that there are just no openings or that the employer isn't hiring at the moment, what you're really being told is you appear to be too average to consider hiring. They can't see value in you. Average is NOT what employers are looking for.

For example, when I ran an advertising agency earlier in my career, a prospect came to me for an interview. We weren't hiring at the time, but I always kept an eye out for new talent anyway. He had a super résumé, but he didn't stop at that. He said, "Mr. Flaum, let's you and me make a deal. If I can't increase this client's business by twenty-five percent in nine months, you don't have to fire me, I'll resign. And I'll put that in writing. That's how sure I am that I can achieve these results for you." Everything about this guy said win-win. So, even though we weren't hiring, I took a chance and hired him on the spot. Not only did he increase our business in the time he said he would—he'd done his due diligence before the interview and knew our client's needs—he also, on his own, brought in two more clients as well.

Realistically, if your résumé and everything else about you says you're an A or A-Plus hire who could really bring value to the organization, you would be hired whether or not there are openings or the company is hiring. A recruiter or employer would be crazy not to hire you! If you come in with an attitude of not only wanting to meet the employer's expectations but also show an eagerness to exceed them, you'll be hired. And if you deliver, you're gold.

You may possibly have to consider moving elsewhere to look for a job or to seize an opportunity. For example, I'm currently mentoring an out-of-work executive who has received a great offer from a company in St. Louis. But she lives on the East Coast and has a family—three young kids in school and a househusband who tends to their children and the home. "I don't think they'd take much to the idea of being uprooted like that," she told me.

What I then suggested, and what many people in this position do, was not to say "no" right away, but to consider the option of relocating in part—flying to St. Louis for a four- or five-day workweek and taking an inexpensive single room or apartment to live in, going home weekends and holidays. "Well, I don't think my husband would be too happy with that arrangement either," she said. And I said, "Maybe so. But don't tell me there are no jobs out there for you."

There's always a way to make things work. You go where the opportunities are. You get the education and training you need. You research the possible employer and come up with one or two really good ideas that the business can use. And you tune out the talking heads and politicians on television, the radio, or the web who keep telling you, for whatever reason, there is no work at all to be had out there. There is always a way to make things work. That's what courageous and successful people do.

Myth #7: "I have to be perfect, and I can't be."

Do you know anyone who's perfect (except in her or his own mind)? We all have faults. What job winners do is they own up to their faults; they open up about them and talk about them, often with a healthy dose of self-deprecating humor.

I was really looking forward to meeting you today, if only to tell you I've got a strike against me from the get-go. I've only had one job to date and am the poster child for Steady Eddie.

I'm a workaholic. I can't even leave my laptop at home when I go on vacation! I spend most of my time trying to hide it from my husband under a beach towel.

It's OK to admit your imperfections—even to recruiters and in job interviews. For example, if a recruiter or potential employer said to you, "If I were to ask your former boss or associates what were your biggest weakness and your biggest asset, what would they say?" A so-called "perfectionist" would likely respond with a litany of assets and no weaknesses and not be believed. He or she would be told, "Thank you for coming in" and politely shown the door.

On the other hand, consider a candidate who says something like this: "Well, I think they would say my greatest weakness is probably impatience. If I have a deadline, I'll push to beat it, even if that involves keeping my staff up all night, which is not always the best move—even if born of a good motive."

That's just honesty—provided it's true, of course, and your former employer and colleagues don't come back with "He's a nag and a tyrant who's always looking over your shoulder, which is why we never get anything done!" Believe me, your answer will be checked out! Expect it, so rehearse what you will say, and turn your lemons into lemonade.

Where does this myth of the need to be perfect come from? Perhaps from a boss who insisted on perfection from others because of his own low personal and professional self-esteem? Or from parents who kept drilling into you as a child how perfect you were, or should have been, and so you grew up still paying the price of their unrealistic expectations?

It's a myth. Nobody's perfect. NOBODY!

Myth #8: "Change is too frightening for me to handle!"

Ever notice a cat walk into a room where something unfamiliar has been added or something familiar taken away? The cat inches hesitantly toward the object or now-empty spot, moves closer then steps back, repeating these cautious movements until it is finally sure the new item won't bite or the vacancy doesn't spell danger.

Cats are extremely sensitive to change of any kind, as are we humans. But we can take sensitivity to change a step further by recoiling from it—shivering at the mere sound of the word. Yes, change can be frightening. But it's a myth that you have to face head-on. It's a fear that can and must be overcome if you hope to excel at any level in any job or profession. You must learn to welcome eagerly the new opportunities that change can present.

One year, for my birthday present, my wife and kids chipped in to get me flying lessons. Flying was something I'd never done before, and something I wasn't convinced I even wanted to try. The prospect of doing something totally out of the ordinary, of getting in the cockpit of an airplane and taking it off the ground myself, even with a licensed pilot by my side, was a bit nerve-wracking. Heck, truth be told, even with the instructor next to me at the controls, the lessons were frightening. But I came to love it, and my fear faded. I had achieved something well outside my comfort zone and was now comfortable with it. The same can be true on the job front. If you've been pounding the pavement every day looking for the same kind of work with no success or are stuck in a job you've grown restless with but are fearful of changing because of the unknown, you don't have to buy into the myth that you can't do anything about your fear.

One excellent tip shared with me by recruiters and Human Resources people to help overcome the fear of change, which I've also learned from my own experience, is the following sleight-of-hand trick. Do something completely removed from your comfort zone outside of work (like taking flying lessons or comedy improv classes). Success there may help you cope better at work and may also translate into your being able to move more comfortably outside your comfort zone on a professional level.

RECRUITER'S MEMO

"Fear of change inevitably produces some big changes—unexpected ones that can turn your world upside down again and again and again if you're not careful. You may hate the idea of change, but it's part of life, so you might as well orchestrate it yourself and be your own conductor."

Here's a good example of a sleight-of-hand trick. When a physician friend of mine turned sixty, he was still a good five or six years away from retirement. He had become very dissatisfied with his job but was fearful of retiring as well. Being a doctor for so long, he was unsure how he would be able to handle no longer seeing and helping patients, the part of the job that he enjoys and takes immense satisfaction in.

One weekend, while he and his wife were vacationing upstate, they went to an art museum where he was quite taken with the sculpture exhibits. He'd never tried sculpting, as it was well out of his area of expertise. But he motivated himself to take some classes and found he not only loved doing it, but he was even good at it!

Not long after, he found that doing something creative away from work, something he'd never even considered, was enabling him to roll with the punches more easily at work and to cope better with other responsibilities that drained him. Now, he no longer fears closing the door on that part of his life when he retires at sixty-six. In fact, he's looking forward to it and to sculpting full time!

Learn from him and do something that may help you feel less in a rut and more enthusiastic at your job or that can give you the courage—and the juice—to go after something different and better.

Learn to embrace change, not be frightened of it. Consider that the next chapter of your life could be extraordinarily rewarding and full of fun.

Myth #9: "Finding something new is too daunting and overwhelming a task."

Like so many employment-related myths I'm exposing here, this one also is rooted more in emotion than in fact.

Let's assume you are in manufacturing and your boss tells you to create plans for a much-needed new plant and to deliver those plans to her in two weeks. How much confidence or can-do attitude you have plays a primary role in whether you can achieve this outcome or not. If your immediate reaction is, "It's too daunting and overwhelming a task. No way can I get it done in two weeks," the likelihood is you won't be able to. On the other hand, if you react as an A-Plus leader with the attitude, "Well, if it has to be done in two weeks, it'll be done in two weeks," the likelihood is that you will achieve that outcome—or come close enough to more than please your boss.

You will get the assignment done by picking the brains of the best people from among your associates, thoughtfully and efficiently parceling out the work, and pacing yourself and others by setting daily goals. It's as simple as that, regardless of the challenge.

However, if you are inherently frightened by the idea of tackling anything, be it a tight schedule or a pending job interview that requires you to play your A-Plus game, then your real issue probably relates to a fear of inadequacy—you feel that you are just not good enough to be able to pull it off. Whatever the reason—you've never done it before, you're facing a challenging assignment in a compressed time frame, you need to impress in a job interview—you feel inadequate to the task because it requires you to move out of your comfort zone to achieve it (the old "change is frightening" bugaboo).

Workers with high self-esteem always look to surround themselves with people who are as smart and capable as they are, or perhaps smarter and even more capable in areas where they are deficient. Certainly the best leaders, those who excel at any job at any level, do this because they know it's the key to real strength, to real productivity, to getting things done the right way.

Those in the workplace with low self-esteem are referred to in the business world as "shade trees." Their feelings of inadequacy are so strong, their egos so fragile, they can't allow anyone else to receive credit but themselves. For them, everything is too daunting and overwhelming a task, and when work does get done (typically by others), they bask in the success, while casting a shadow over everyone else. However, such people seldom rise in any organization and, if they do, they seldom last. So, if this is you, be warned and get to work on it...or be gone!

Myth #10: "I'm too chunky, too short, too awkward, too talkative, or inarticulate."

A friend of mine, whom I won't name for fear of embarrassing her, is considered by all who know her to be one of the best and brightest head honchos in business today, as well as one of the most self-effacing. She hadn't intended a career in business. She wanted to be a history teacher, but after college, she found herself working in market research at an automotive firm and rose up the ranks from there.

To everyone who's ever worked with and for her over the years, she's always been a great mentor and a role model for what a leader can and should be. To my knowledge, she has never taken personal credit for her many achievements but has instead always bestowed the praise on others. Her employees adore her. They work their butts off for her just because it's her.

This woman has such a high degree of self-confidence that she doesn't need to show it. She conveys confidence naturally and is a skilled hand at showing confidence in others' abilities. She's always been this way, her family tells me, having followed throughout her career many of the precepts you're reading about in this book—which I learned from HER!

However, here's the twist. At first sight, no one in central casting would ever consider her for the part of a top-level CEO. She's short. She's no athlete (from early on, she says). And she's on the portly side of chunky (she admits to having had a weight problem all her life). In other words, she will tell you with a smile, she doesn't have the *Elle* look that many executives and CEOs strive for.

But here's the next twist: No one she's worked for or who works for her sees this when they're with her. What they see is a sharp, articulate, self-confident, high-level performer and listener with superb leadership qualities.

If chunky, short, awkward, inarticulate, or talkative is what you see when you look in the mirror, others will see that too. In the work world, it's not what they see that determines how you perform and bring out your best, but what you see. In a sense this is true of all the myths I've explored in this chapter. But, fortunately, these myths are the easiest obstacles to overcome precisely because they are myths. They are just paper-thin roadblocks that can swiftly be brushed aside.

The more troublesome saboteurs possess thornier symptoms that reflect deeper, more stubborn, but no less conquerable, issues. In the next chapter I'll reveal these four saboteurs and, in Chapter 3, show you how to transform these negative behaviors into positive action.

Chapter 2

The Four Stages of Sabotaging Yourself

"I have a tendency to sabotage relationships; I have a tendency to sabotage everything. Fear of success, fear of failure, fear of being afraid. Useless, good-for-nothing thoughts."
-- Michael Bublé, Canadian Vocalist and Songwriter

Mark was the regional manager of a large food store chain in the Northeast. Tragedy struck when he and his wife experienced the loss of child. Mark went into such an emotional tailspin that, within two years, his marriage collapsed and he lost his job.

Mark believed that burying himself in a new job as quickly as possible was the best antidote for all the pain he was feeling, and so ready, in his own mind at least, to take on a new role, he sought help from recruitment firms to arrange job interviews.

To Mark's surprise, but not to that of the recruiters—or to friends who knew him well—Mark failed abysmally in interview after interview. The off-the-record feedback to the recruiters from the potential employers was almost universally the same. Employers reported that Mark's energy level at these interviews ranged between flat to desperate. But the recruiters' debriefs of Mark himself following these interviews yielded a very different perception. Mark believed that each had gone exceptionally well and said he expected to be called back quickly by one or more of these employers with a firm job offer.

Mark wasn't trying to deceive the recruiters. He truly felt this way; he actually believed what he was saying. All the losses he had recently suffered had left him with such feelings of anger and betrayal—issues not dealt with—that he had sunk into a state of depression that clouded his judgment and rendered him unable to see things clearly anymore.

Mark needed the support of family, friends, former associates—perhaps even psychological help—to help pull him out of this dangerous malaise and get him back on track with clarity and purpose. Consumed by his anger and a desire to get even with the world, he initially resisted: "I don't need anybody; I can handle this on my own!" But then, as he approached rock bottom, he finally saw the light and recognized his need. He reached out to family and friends. He entered therapy to help deal with his depression, anger, and other issues. He also resumed contact with his network of former colleagues and other business associates.

Today Mark is a much happier man. He has a good job in retail management. And, just recently, he's become engaged.

As we can see from this true story that a recruiter friend related to me for this book, circumstances, psychological factors, and our attitudes all fuel how we attack the job market in the wake of a career setback—especially when that setback combines with other issues and turmoil going on in our lives, as it almost invariably does. Being able early on to recognize and identify these circumstances, psychological factors, and attitudes so that we can overcome them is essential to being effective in a job search.

It is also the step that most how-tos on job hunting in the wake of a frustrated career or career reversal tend to ignore. I call these circumstances, psychological factors, and attitudes—all of them key inhibitors to meeting with success in the job market—the "four stages of sabotaging yourself." The stages are anger, recrimination, depression, and unfocused and unproductive behavior.

When faced with being out of work on top of all his other problems, Mark eventually fell prey to all of these saboteurs, because not addressing each allowed one to metastasize into the next. But Mark was lucky. He found ways to combat them and to stop sabotaging himself (as you will too in Chapter 3).

Not everyone is as lucky as Mark. So, let's take a close look at each of these saboteurs and see if you recognize them in anyone— even yourself, perhaps.

1. Anger

Symptoms: "Why me?" "What they're saying is bull!" "They're not fair; I can't stand them!"
Result: Will consume most of your waking hours, if permitted, and lead to recrimination.

Anger manifests itself differently depending upon the career reversal you've experienced. Being outright fired, downsized, or laid off are obviously the worst, of course, because they're not only major blows to your self-worth but also to your pocketbook. In all cases, you're out of a job. You may have mouths to feed, children to educate, and definitely bills to pay. Unemployment insurance isn't enough to get you through. Under such circumstances, it is only natural to feel anger and resentment toward your former employer and the fates in general, not to mention some envy toward those who are still employed.

To be passed over for an important promotion (especially one that has been promised to you) can be a heavy blow to your self-worth, leaving you feeling angry, demoralized, and bitter. But, let's face it, at least you're still employed. The same is true if you're stuck in a dead-end job. You may feel angry, resentful, and lower than a sperm whale's belly button. You may go home every night seething and miserable, but you do have the relative compensation of knowing you can still collect a paycheck, even if you hate going to "that hellish place" to earn it or hate having to make nice to that supervisor you can't stand.

Where anger moves into self-sabotage territory and becomes dangerous is when you permit anger to overtake you, and you allow it to become a full-time job. Constantly stoking the fires of anger keeps you from being able to move away from it and leads to focusing on all the wrong things.

"Here's what we've learned from working with job candidates if they can't let go of their anger," a top recruiter tells me. "It becomes a viral coat to cover hurt and fear. Left unchecked, it presents itself in business interactions and job interviews—perhaps most especially then—as a disease.

"Walk into a room for any interaction, such as an interview for employment, a meeting, a presentation, and everyone there can't help but feel the heat of anger coming off them. As the failed interviews, meetings, and presentations inevitably build up, the virus becomes more profound. The viral cycle gains momentum, the anger grows, hurt and fear build, and self-esteem becomes as compromised as an immune system."

The prescription for anger, she concludes, is to "Hang up the coat; look at every inch of it, no matter how much it hurts; deal with it; and then leave it tucked away in the closet before entering into any further interactions. If you don't, you lose. If you do, you will win."

I'll go into how to combat anger and convert it to positive action in Chapter 3, but for now, I'll just say that she's right. The worst thing you can do with anger is to keep feeding it. And when looking for a job or trying to better yourself in any way professionally, if your emotional immune system becomes compromised, you will tend to place emphasis where emphasis doesn't belong, and you will make mistakes and snap decisions that only wind up costing you more than you will gain.

For example, a colleague of mine, who worked at the pharmaceutical company that stiffed me on my promised promotion, was subsequently let go when the company downsized. He'd been there for many years (as I had) and was angry that some coworkers with less seniority had been kept on. His anger festered into an open emotional wound that obscured his judgment, prompting him to grab the first job offer that came his way at a small advertising agency in New Jersey. "There! That'll show 'em!" he said without any joy at being employed again, but with bitterness and defiance.

He soon realized that he had made a big mistake taking this job so quickly. He wasn't suited to it at all or with dealing with his crusty new CEO. He became so miserable that, angry with himself now, he made yet another rash decision: he up and quit. He told himself that he would have enough to live on if he sold some stock he owned, and so, he said, "The hell with everybody. I just won't work!"

And for all I know, he has kept to his word. The last time I saw him he had put on so much weight from doing nothing—except eating apparently—that I barely recognized him. I eventually lost track of him.

Unlike Mark in the previous story, this fellow let his anger over losing his job go so unchecked that the other saboteurs soon overtook him as well, eventually crippling him, not just on a professional level but a personal one as well.

RECRUITER'S MEMO

"A candidate had been laid off from two companies in a row after the crash of 2009. The way her anger showed up in the interview process was through righteous indignation, revealed by her stiff, unsmiling face and unrelaxed body language. It was fully apparent that she was angry and placed the blame on her former employers. Throughout each interview, she was angry, and never being called back, she felt her indignation growing in every subsequent interview. Finally facing facts, she took three months off from interviewing to heal body, mind, and soul. Five months from the time she decided to take this path, she had two competing job offers with a third offer on the way."

2. Recrimination

<u>Symptoms</u>: "How can I get even with those SOBs?" "I know their dirty secrets!" "I'll tell everyone what goes on."
<u>Result</u>: A totally inefficient and wasteful use of energy and time that leads to depression.

It was certainly nothing I did!

It was the company culture!

My boss is just an inept idiot...but he's close to the CEO.

It's not surprising we try to put the best spin possible on why we were let go or passed over. For one thing, this form of self-justification is part and parcel of the process of coping with the blow to our pride. So, in trying to cast the best possible light on us and, where possible, the worst on them, we may shade the truth a bit at a job interview; it makes us feel like we're not culpable and are evening up the score, at least a little. But lies can pop out too if you're not careful. This will happen if you allow yourself to be eaten up with thoughts of recrimination, and the professional damage that results may be permanent.

"I was doing a great job for that company, and then wham! They tell me I'm history. They didn't want to move into the new territory I had mapped out, and it would have saved them. They're an ungrateful bunch of egomaniacs. No guts, no glory!" spills out during a job interview when you're asked why you were let go or why you are looking for a better job. It's not likely or believable that your former employer was out to get you or that everyone on top was hopelessly inept, but let's say you weren't exaggerating. How will the interviewer—either a recruiter or a potential employer—react?

RECRUITER'S MEMO

"We quickly dismiss candidates who verbally bad-mouth their ex-bosses. Why? Who's to say they won't do it again?"

The perception is that you can't be trusted to accurately assess a situation wherever you'll work next, and that you may wind up bad-mouthing that company too. And so, even with your anger justified, you don't get the job. Unfair? Yes, but this is the real world of recruitment and employment I'm writing about here, not a fairy tale version where everything turns out right and everyone lives happily ever after.

RECRUITER'S MEMO

"I remember being interviewed as a much younger man in my twenties. I had just left a consulting firm and I was angry about how they handled it. Although I was well qualified for the new opportunity and I felt they had a sincere interest, I did not get an offer. A few years later I met the interviewer again. He told me I had invested so much time during the interview trashing my former employer that he felt I was not ready to focus on the new opportunity, even though he felt I was a good fit. This was a valuable insight for me both professionally and personally then and in later years."

Here's another stinging reality of the world of work involving recrimination, even when it takes the worthy form of whistle-blowing. The recruiter for the company or organization where you're seeking work—and/or their Human Resources department—will check you out thoroughly (and I don't mean just your references).

Believe me, if you blew the whistle on or filed a suit against your former employer—no matter how well justified it may have been—a recruiter's or employer's reaction often times will be "Don't call us, and we'll never call you." In fact, you'd better hope to get a hefty settlement to sustain you into retirement because it's unlikely you'll ever be hired by anyone ever again. No matter how well suited you may be for the job, your interviewers will see a sign stuck on your forehead that reads "DISLOYAL!" And, undeniably, there are prospective employers who empathize with the whistle-blower's employer and think *If she did this to them, she could do it to us.*

Here's what a top recruiter recently shared with me: "There are unspoken realities a candidate experiences when he or she has entered into the abyss of doing the right thing as a whistle-blower," she said. "One reality is that while many admire the courage of the whistle-blower, a distancing effect occurs between would-be champions and coworkers—even those supporting a whistle-blower's job-seeking efforts. Fear of being identified with the whistle-blower can be perceived as a career-limiting factor, if not a danger.

"This is particularly noticeable in fragile and unforgiving economic times when there are more job seekers than jobs available. While the law may protect the whistle-blower, human behavior, specifically fear, does not. Whistle-blowers often experience business relationships to be like walking on eggshells.

Those who have filed a discrimination action against a previous employer often encounter the same experiences."

She advises, "Your best shot at any upside from either of these scenarios is to take the chance and tell the truth, up front and proactively, during the interview process. Having a prospective employer find out via reference checking or background checks negates the opportunity to own control of managing your own message, both fairly and accurately. But you can't do that if you're swallowed up by recrimination."

She continues, "The bottom line is it's irrelevant that you're well within your legal right to protect yourself from discrimination. There is a vast chasm between what is well within one's legal right and the responsive fear and bias of 'This could happen to us too.' The candidate will not be told this is why there is an abrupt cooling of the relationship with no job offer on the horizon, but it's there. In essence, recrimination becomes the painful gift that just keeps on giving."

RECRUITER'S MEMO

"You leave a company—dismissed or otherwise—and you tell the recruiter or a prospective employer why you left. The recruiter or employer then calls your ex-employer's HR department, or your former boss, or a former coworker, or a member or a friend on the board of directors to get the real scoop. Why do they do this? Because you look like a shady character? No. It's because even those not consumed by the recrimination bug tend to paint themselves in the most favorable light. In other words, you had better be sure your explanation and the real scoop jibe."

3. Depression

Symptoms: Disillusionment, lowering of self-esteem, sadness.
Result: Immobilization, leading to unfocused and unproductive behavior.

A friend in broadcasting told me this story. He worked in the Midwest at what is called in the business an "O and O," a local television station "owned and operated" by a major network. The station was going through some management turmoil at the time.

One Friday afternoon, shortly before 5 p.m., his immediate boss was called into the general manager's office for an impromptu meeting. My friend later ran into his boss emerging from the GM's office, as he was coming down the hall. "His face was ashen," my friend described him. "He looked sick—either that or shell-shocked. I stopped and asked him what was wrong. He didn't even look at me. He just kept walking, heading for the exit to the parking lot, muttering, in a voice that was toneless and without life, just three words as he went by: 'They fired me.' I'll never forget his face when he said that. Anguished is too mild a description. I'm not sure he was even thinking about what he was going to do or how he would support his family. At that moment, he just looked beyond dejected—he looked as if he had lost everything."

This is how many men—and women too, but more so men—immediately react upon being given the heave-ho by an employer. The reaction is also the same when men and women receive bad news related to their job, such as, "You know that job you were in line for? Well, I'm sorry to say we've decided to give it to someone else."

To male ears, that message usually comes across as "Someone

who is more skilled than you are, better looking, plays to the top, and has a more winning personality has gotten the promotion." This is because men tend to equate their self-worth with their jobs to a higher degree than many women do. And if you place that much emphasis on your job as a measure of who you are, it's almost inevitable that losing it or being passed over will come as a crushing blow. It doesn't matter what the circumstances are either.

My friend said that his boss was let go as a result of consolidation in a management power grab. In other words, his firing was purely political Didn't matter; the fellow was devastated. Maybe it's the old hunter-gatherer instinct bred into men as a species many millions of years ago that is offended. But that's how we are. We men have fragile egos.

If you don't deal with whatever degree of depression you're feeling from the blow to your professional self-worth, what happens is this. The lowering of your self-esteem combines with chronic sadness and disillusionment to paint a dismal picture of the world with everybody in it out to get you. You start bemoaning the fact that you haven't heard from your sister. "She knows what I'm going through!" Or that your children away at college haven't called. "They know I've lost my job. Is it too much to ask that they check in with me once in a while to see how I'm doing?"

We can't realistically expect family, friends, and colleagues to drop everything in their lives and spend time with us under these circumstances, and yet that's what we come to expect of them. They may even be calling and checking in with us regularly to see how we're doing and to help bolster our spirits. But it's not enough, because our depression has blown everything way out of proportion.

People who stay in jobs they hate are perfect candidates for sustained depression. The boss is an SOB, or the work is unsatisfying and not nearly as financially rewarding as it needs to be. But they feel they just have to grin and bear it for the sake of their income, health care, and the welfare of their family. They become less productive, and at their next performance review, they're told they're not meeting expectations, so they pick up the pace because they're scared of losing the very job they've come to hate, which fuels their hatred, depression, and resentment even more. And that's the state they're in when they go home every night.

RECRUITER'S MEMO

"Depression sets in as part of a chronic continuum of hurt and fear that are left to run amok. One of the first signs that should serve as a wake-up call that depression is present is when one says, 'I have to go to an interview,' not, 'I get to go to an interview.' The day you don't approach each new job interview feeling nervous yet eager, like being on a first date, is the day to check your depression temperature. Depression is insidious. It creeps into people and, as a result, into every aspect of their thinking and behavior. If you're stuck in a job you hate, this can be especially damaging, not only to you but also to your coworkers and the workplace environment as a whole. If depression is not dealt with, the healthy employee and healthy workplace environment can be lost."

Not surprisingly, temporary release from depression takes many forms. People will start blowing their tops a lot at home— at their spouse, partners, the kids, the family dog, whoever's handy. Relationships begin to suffer. People may look elsewhere for other things to make them happy—perhaps having an affair. It happens all the time. Or they may take the opposite approach and decide to spend every free minute with family (more quality time, they will say), which is fine, up to a point. But if the family starts feeling suffocated by the constant togetherness, it's not so fine.

Also, for men and, I suspect, long-in-the-job women—who both put so much emphasis on their jobs as a measure of their self-worth—more quality time with the family or buddies often doesn't compensate sufficiently for the damage done to their bruised egos. Yes, it's good to strive for balance between our work and home lives—we could all use more of it. But a gratifying, fulfilling job is part of that balance, and that can't be achieved, or even sought after, when depression obscures all but the most negative thoughts and actions.

4. Unfocused And Unproductive Behavior

Symptoms: Living in the past twenty-four hours a day.
Result: Uncertainty, lack of productivity, anxiety, continued anger, and prolonged unemployment.

We've all known people who have suffered an employment reversal of some kind and, having never quite bounced back from that reversal, seem stuck in replay mode. Ask them about anything—the time of day, politics, the weather, sports, or just how they're doing—and almost inevitably they will steer the conversation back to what they want to talk about most: how they were let go "oh so unfairly," didn't get that promotion they were "oh so qualified" for, or if it hadn't been for "[fill in the blanks]," they would've, could've, should've "been promoted," "gotten that bonus," "moved up to the A team."

This obsession with the past is the ultimate by-product of failing to deal with anger, the first of our four self-saboteurs. You get stuck. And you can't seem to get unstuck and move forward because what got you stuck in the first place now occupies your every waking moment. You can't plan for the future because that represents change, and you hate change—especially because of what change has already visited upon you. And so you're not motivated to try turning things around, because it has become more comfortable, and comforting, to keep dwelling on the past.

This is unfocused and unproductive behavior and, arguably, the most dangerous of the four saboteurs, because it represents the end of the line. If you let this saboteur rule as you've done with the previous three, the chances are you won't ever recover and get the job you've always wanted. You won't have to worry about looking for a job, networking with colleagues for leads, developing relationships with recruiters, or wondering how in a job interview to communicate the added value you feel you can bring to a potential employer, because you will likely never get the opportunity. After a while even the most receptive ears that were willing to listen to you—those of family members and friends—will likely shut down: "Oh, no, if he brings up that again I think I'll scream!"

This type of shutdown is what can happen if you remain stuck in the past rather than seeking to correct course and chart a more productive path to the future. Instead of getting even with a former employer by doing better, you just continue to languish in your own self-made limbo.

Very early in my career, just after I'd gotten out of the Army, I worked as head of public relations for a New York radio station. Two people younger than I reported to me. Maybe because I was still acting in military mode (pay attention to detail!), I was tough on them, particularly on execution. Eventually they complained to the general manager and I lost my job. Here I thought I was just doing my best to get the job done, and I'd been fired for it!

This sort of setback never comes at a good time, but the timing here was particularly bad. My former wife was pregnant with our first child and the loss of my job meant the loss of my health benefits. I needed another job quick! I applied for the first one that came my way—a public relations position at a nonprofit located in Miami.

I went down there for the interview and to look things over, and while I was there my head cleared long enough for me to be able to see that this job wasn't for me and that the top-down, command-and-control management style was a poor technique for generating growth. Realizing THAT was the beginning of my turnaround and helped me to regain focus.

Returning to New York, I was recruited into public affairs for a pharmaceutical company. I liked public relations a lot, but my goal was to get into marketing. However, I had no credentials. So, on the side, I decided to go after my MBA from Fairleigh Dickinson University in New Jersey under the GI Bill. Those four years of working during the day and going to school in the evening and on weekends were rough, but good things happened as a result to keep me from falling back into the groove of living in the past.

You can combat unfocused and unproductive behavior and the three other saboteurs too. There are proven ways not to keep falling into the traps set by them and techniques to motivate you into transforming whatever job or career reversal you've experienced into determination. You can move on, forgive your own errors, make the best of your situation, and go after the job you've always wanted. Adopt as your mantra always to move forward in life, personally and professionally.

In Chapter 3, I'll show you how to overcome these four deadly saboteurs and convert them into positive actions to help kick-start and design the next exciting chapter in your working life.

RECRUITER'S MEMO

"Focus is a precious, valuable 'F-word.' History continues to teach us that unfocused candidates seeking jobs remain unemployed. 'Un' in front of 'focused' or 'employed' is not a good thing. You must get the 'un' out of your job search or career climb, and start thinking 'laser-focus.'"

Chapter 3

How to Combat These Saboteurs

"There are risks and costs to a program of action. But they are far less than the long-range risks and costs of comfortable inaction."
-- John F. Kennedy (1917-1963), 35TH President of the United States

The prime ingredient in being able to fight off the four stages of self-sabotage is facing up to the fact that you're vulnerable to them in the first place. Then, recognize you had better deal with them NOW or risk being held back by their lingering aftereffects for a good long time—maybe permanently.

In the previous chapter, you learned what these hurtful saboteurs are and how to recognize them. In this chapter, you will learn how to convert their negative impact into positive action, using recommended tips and techniques to pull you out of your funk.

This chapter is all about attitude and commitment: the attitude to work harder and be smarter than your peers in the competitive job market and the commitment to create your own momentum in getting the job or promotion you now crave.

1. Convert Anger To Positive Action

<u>Primary Objective</u>: Confront your anger, open up about your anger, and start moving ahead by releasing it.

Generally, women tend to be more willing to open up and talk freely about their problems than are men. Men who are angry about an employment setback tend to interiorize their anger and carry it for a much longer period of time. The reason for this difference, therapists maintain, is that in a crisis situation—and a job loss or languishing in a job one hates certainly qualifies—women will often confide in family, friends, and colleagues. They are also more willing to seek professional therapy in an effort to quickly manage and resolve the crisis. But men often like to stew in their own juices for a bit, lamenting the "unfairness of it all," even though such behavior is not only counterproductive but also self-destructive.

I've seen examples of these two very different types of responses when counseling clients and friends rebounding from a career setback. The guys are inclined to wallow longer in their anger and hurt, even though they are sharp go-getters who clearly should know better. Conversely, the women let off steam fairly quickly and disperse it rather than have it boil up inside them until it implodes or explodes. Perhaps we men should strive to be more like women in this regard. Hmm...

One very important reason for getting rid of anger from a blow to self-esteem is that it shows even when you think you are doing a great job covering it up. Here's how one of the sharpest recruiters in the business describes the professional fallout that can occur from being and staying angry.

"People who remain terribly angry about losing their jobs typically don't even know how many opportunities they are missing," he says. "The highest performing teams and individuals pride themselves on how quickly they extinguish and redirect their negative energy. These people have learned that anger and other negative and isolating emotions at work, or when looking for work, are disadvantages to them. It is important to recognize what sets off your trigger so you can learn to redirect and harness that negative energy. Ultimately, uncontrolled anger only leads to missed opportunities and strained, inefficient relationships."

RECRUITER'S MEMO

"Looking for a job is an Olympic event. You don't get do-overs. It requires that your best, your fairest, your most earnest (not desperate!), yet most competitive game be on."

Angry people (especially men), looking for work or hoping to get a better job, actually will go to interviews with recruiters and employers with a noticeable chip on their shoulder, a Human Resources expert tells me. "All they want to talk about is themselves and how unfairly they were treated by their former employer, or how misunderstood they are by their current one, or how badly the company is being managed," he explains. "That kind of behavior is a real no-no. The focus of the job search, especially at the interview stage, should always be on the potential employer, the positives you can bring to the company or the position, and what ultimately you can do for that employer. The focus should not be on what a past employer has done to you. It seems like common sense. And it is. But angry people don't do it. They remain eaten up by fury, and it comes through."

RECRUITER'S MEMO

"If I detect any sign of anger in a job candidate, he or she doesn't stand a chance with me, no matter how good his or her reputation and résumé may be. If candidates haven't managed to change their attitude, I won't recommend them to my employer-clients because I'll look bad letting someone like them through their door."

Blowing up at your spouse, the kids, the dog, your friends, or a recruiter is not the way to release your anger over a job crisis. But release it you must in order to move forward successfully.

My advice is to take action quickly by seeking out a mentor—a wiser and definitely cooler head—among your closest and most successful business friends, colleagues, or family. Call upon old bosses for their advice, ones you can talk to and with whom you have a long-standing relationship. They make excellent mentors. Confide your bitterness, sense of betrayal, and frayed self-respect to your mentor. Expose your anger to him or her—a safe place where venting won't do you any harm. A good mentor will allow you to start releasing yourself from anger's grip.

I am currently mentoring two longtime colleagues who sought me out expressly for this purpose. One is in his forties, the other in his fifties. Both were senior level executives when they lost their jobs, and both are extraordinarily angry over what's happened to them. They feel they were treated unfairly.

I've counseled each of them to feel free to express their anger by letting it go on me. "For your sake and that of your family and career, you can't remain in this negative state of mind," I tell them. "You've got to become more positive so that you can move forward, and getting rid of your anger is the first step. If telling me how angry you are helps you start doing that, so much the better."

I've also recommended they try a form of meditation, which I and others have used, that has helped defuse us in an employment crisis. Here's what you do. For a few minutes each morning after you've gotten up, place a pillow on the floor and sit on it cross-legged. Keeping your mouth shut, breathe evenly through your nose while keeping your mind as free as possible to achieve a state of pure relaxation. It's hard to do at first, but with practice it becomes much easier, and you will be amazed at how much this simple exercise will eventually help free you from your rage.

Strenuous exercise at your local YMCA or your fitness center several times a week or quiet time sitting in the steam room on a regular basis may help you achieve a similar result. Whatever it takes, do it! And as the anger dissipates, you will begin to feel more positive and open to taking aggressive action in the right direction rather than the wrong one.

2. Convert Recrimination To Outshining Your Rejecters

<u>Primary Objective</u>: Exceed your own expectations by moving beyond "I'll get even with those SOBs" to "I'll drive this new job opportunity and become more successful than any of them!"

Success is the best revenge. I don't know who first said that, but it's true.

When I failed to get the promotion I'd been promised, after eighteen years of dedicated service launching new divisions and products that dramatically increased revenues for my pharmaceutical employer, I was not just shattered and angry—but out for revenge. *How can I get even with them for doing this to me?* That question consumed me, until I realized that the best way to settle the score was to become more successful professionally than anybody still working there and to do it quickly and on my own terms. It wasn't about money, it was about accomplishments.

This realization, and the decisions I made after that, may never have occurred, however, had I not converted my anger and desire for revenge into positive action. I transformed them into a motivating force: fuel that spurred me to take action and exceed my own career expectations.

"Hey, I'm good!" I told myself. "My past job performance is uncontested. I deserve better recognition and I'm going to get it!"

That is the spark that led me to achieving everything I have set out to do since. And I was able to make it all happen because I made myself exchange that early goal to simply get even for a more positive one—to do better by surpassing my rejecters.

Six months after I had left the company, I finally managed to take stock of myself and came to the conclusion that the company had simply missed out on a great opportunity by not doing right by me. I was feeling very good about my prospects and myself again, and as a result, good things started to break my way.

And to my surprise, I was even contacted by the chairman of my former pharmaceutical company who offered me the very position I'd been denied. "We made a big mistake," he confessed. *You bet you did*, I thought as I turned him down, not because I wished to savor the act of getting even—which would only have been spiteful—but because I had decisively moved on in my own mind and heart. I couldn't go back, not if I wanted to achieve my goal of doing better. So that meant I had to keep moving forward.

RECRUITER'S MEMO

"When you come to us speaking in glowing terms about your former employer, does that raise our suspicions that you are too good to be true? NO! What we see is a person with a lot of polish and class, who can say, 'You know, I made some mistakes there, and so did they, but it's a great firm with very good people.' You now sound like a professional instead of somebody with just an axe to grind—however justified it might be."

Employment professionals, such as recruiters and Human Resources personnel, confirm that someone who comes to them harboring the desire to get even with a former employer (or anyone else for that matter) will never get past their desk.

Their belief is that people don't wander too far from their roots in terms of past behavior. For example, if you are the who's hard to deal with because you always have to be right and who can't bring up any positives about the progress of the team, can you blame them for concluding you'll be that way in your next job too? So, no surprise, they'll veto you right away.

In working with job seekers, I've found this conclusion and its inevitable consequences to be accurate. Recently, I've been trying to help a bit of an intense guy who was up for the general manager of a midsized manufacturing firm before he was unceremoniously let go. Problem was nobody wanted to work with him and, as a result, the company was losing a lot of good people from his team. He's definitely smart and he did well for the company financially, but he had the reputation of being a tyrannical prima donna on the job, and he carries it still.

It's a tough situation. He's been out of work for over a year and the interviews are drying up fast because his attempts to describe himself as a team-player while blaming his team only confirms the reputation he has. Recruiters and potential employers, who perform due diligence in researching this candidate's background, believe that chances are he'll stay true to his character, no matter what spin he puts on his past behavior.

RECRUITER'S MEMO

"Most references we see from candidates are bulls**t. Unless we pry, we never get the full picture. That's why good recruiters and cautious employers don't go just with the references they're given. We go beyond these references and talk to the candidate's old bosses, coworkers, and peers, asking them point-blank whether they would hire or want to work with the individual again, and why (or why not.)"

One savvy recruiter I know advises this way: "While it's never a good idea to burn bridges, sometimes losing a job or feeling you were treated unfairly, like being passed over for a promotion, can cause people to react in ways they wouldn't normally," she says. "However, it's a very small world out there, and so people should be very careful about how they react when receiving bad news.

"Yes, I do believe, particularly in this day and age of the Internet and with forums like Twitter, Facebook, and Glassdoor, folks have to be very careful about what they say, write, and do. Everything leaves a mark. In ink. So mouthing off when you're angry or upset might stay with you a lot longer than it did years ago. It's important to recognize that you should seek to control the things you can control and let go of the things you can't."

The capacity to surpass your rejecters requires not just that you move beyond your anger and recrimination but also that you maintain a courteous and professional relationship with your former employer and, if possible, a cordial one. If you are let go (for whatever reason), be sure to ask for an explanation in writing. This is called a termination letter and should fully explain the reason for your leaving and should be written in mutually agreed-upon language. Offer to word the termination letter yourself or ask to review the letter and rework the company's words, if necessary.

Likewise, if you are continually passed over for promotions, don't ignore what you are feeling and abruptly quit or, worse, stew angrily about it until you decide to move on. Ask why you are being passed over and get the explanation in writing—again in mutually agreed-upon language—before making any decisions. What you find out may actually help you get that promotion or may help you learn the truth about why you are never going to advance there. If the explanation smells of unfairness, you'll have the confirmation of it in writing.

The key is this: however a termination letter is created, it should be agreed to and signed by both parties—that means you, your former boss, and/or the Human Resources department's representative. If you have a termination letter, you can worry a lot less about raising a recruiter's or potential employer's antennae when applying for a job. When you're asked for an explanation of why you left or were let go, just offer up the letter and leave it at that.

Sample Termination Letter

To Whom It May Concern,

The following letter explains the reason for the departure of (Name) from (Company).

(Company), as you may be aware, has experienced a fairly significant downsizing over the past twelve months. (Name) was a department e-Marketing director for three years and we were pleased, overall, with her performance. In the downsizing, we chose to consolidate two departments and name one e-Marketing head. We decided, after much deliberation, to choose a candidate who has been with us for ten years for that newly created position.

We would recommend (Name) to you for senior IT positions. She is a good supervisor with a good performance record.

Sincerely yours,

(Name / Title)

Search professionals for recruitment organizations and potential employers will appreciate not having to probe as deeply for the real scoop about you. They will be impressed by the professional behavior you showed by soliciting this letter and by how your former employer treated you respectfully in return.

Taking positive action is the only way you can avoid being stuck in place wanting only to get even and start on the road to outshining your rejecters.

3. Convert Depression To Motivation

Primary Objective: Start feeling good about yourself again by reaching out for warmth and friendship—even getting therapy to revitalize your energy.

A job loss or other job setbacks are so closely related to the image we have of our own self-worth that feeling good about ourselves again may seem like a tough hill to climb. But climbing it is essential if we hope to be able to bounce back better than ever. This is why I champion the idea of briefly venting angry feelings and then getting back on track as quickly as possible. If you don't, you risk slipping into a state of depression—the epitome of not feeling good about yourself, a condition from which you may find it much slower and more difficult to recover.

Those closest to you—spouse, partner, a good friend—may start drawing away from you if you fail to move out of your funk, which will compound the problem by fueling your depression even more. As I mentioned in Chapter 2, it's never just one thing in a job crisis that will uproot you and throw you into a tailspin. The repercussions from that crisis, plus other unforeseen circumstances and unintended consequences of your behavior, contribute as well.

Relationships may start to crack. Friends who've been supportive may back away. The phone will stop ringing. Job recruiters won't get back to you. Your job queries will meet with no response. And your self-image will plummet as you get down on yourself even more. Your depression will show in your voice, in your body language, in your attitude and actions—everywhere. No employer would consider hiring anyone who exhibits such poor self-esteem. And truth be told: misery may love company, but companies don't love misery.

Feeling good about yourself is a key step in rehabilitating yourself to be able to see the job opportunities that are available for you—a step that's almost impossible to take if you remain angry and depressed. So how do you start feeling good about yourself again under these circumstances? Here are some suggestions that have worked for me and for those I've mentored in getting through such a crisis. Believe me, they work.

RECRUITER'S MEMO

"Why feel good? Once again, the law of attraction is relevant. Real, positive energy invites similar feelings."

You can't begin putting your best foot forward if you don't know which foot this is. So, one of the ways to begin feeling good about yourself again is to do a little self-analysis to find out what makes you tick and what value you bring to others. I recommend creating a series of lists that when tallied up will result in a clear picture of the real you. You can use the following list titles or come up with titles of your own.

What Are My Strengths	What Are My Weaknesses
What I Like About Work	What I Don't Like About Work
What Makes Me Happy	What Makes Me Unhappy
What's Important to Me	What Isn't Important to Me
What Skills Do I Have	What Do I Need to Learn

The goal here is to look inward and rediscover the person worth hiring (and the reasons why) and to reclaim a sense of validation—you have abilities and qualities that are valuable. This exercise is designed to lift you out of your depression by pinpointing the reasons why you're valuable to yourself and to an employer. The exercise will also show you characteristics that may potentially lower your self-esteem.

The results will also prepare you to go after the job or career you've always wanted, because now you will be armed with a better understanding of where you truly shine and in what position, industry, or institution. Knowledge that will enable you to become the most valuable employee of all: an A performer.

If you find yourself getting stuck, reach out to people with good common sense who are close to you personally and/or professionally and ask for their insights. Even if they have started drawing away from you, once they see you're reaching out to them for a reason other than venting, you'll get the honest feedback you're looking for. You will be amazed what this exercise will tell you about yourself and how invaluable, uplifting, and liberating that self-knowledge will be.

For example, what if you are a salesperson and you hate selling, or think that you do? And yet you are a top seller who consistently gets results. Obviously there's something you must like about selling or you wouldn't be so good at it. There must be something else you hate about the job. But what?

Perhaps this exercise in self-analysis will reveal that what you really hate is all the traveling that comes with the job. So maybe the solution then is to find another sales job with a smaller radius where you won't have to spend so many hours on the road. You won't have to give up what you're good at—what makes you an A performer—in order to feel happier, less stressed, and more fulfilled.

On the other hand, maybe you'll find out that you are in the wrong job, business, or field entirely and that this is holding you back from becoming an A performer.

I knew a woman who worked in marketing for a nonprofit organization. She worked her tail off to get the organization's fund-raising numbers up, but eventually she fell out with her despotic and overbearing boss and was let go. She reached out to me for some advice on what she should do and where she should go. During our conversation, I got her to respond to a verbal checklist designed to find out what her real issues were.

"Is this the kind of work you want to keep on doing?" I asked her.

"I don't know," she replied after a long pause. "I mean, I like marketing; it's the fund-raising I can't stand." That was the crux of it. Her tyrannical, overbearing boss wasn't even an issue with her. She had the right talents, but for the wrong job. Consumer marketing was more her thing than nonprofit fund-raising. So that's the door she decided to go through—a door she might not have even considered had she not been fired and then urged to evaluate herself and look at other options more closely.

If you are in the wrong job or field, you are simply not motivated to become an A or A-Plus performer. Passion for the work you do is what really separates the A performer from lesser performers. Whatever the profession, if you lose your job, can't progress, or find yourself growing stale, ask yourself, "Is this right for me?"

Your answer will tell you a lot about whether you really have the fire to do what's required to become an A or A-Plus performer in that job or profession.

You need to know what makes you happy or unhappy, satisfied or dissatisfied in order to be able to reach the level you seek. If you're a lawyer and you hate lawyering, you'll never be a top lawyer. It's a simple as that. The same goes for any profession: finance, information technology, education, health care, scientific research, carpentry, painting—you name it. If you don't feel good about what you do, and how you go about doing it, you won't feel good about yourself and so will never graduate to A-Plus performer status. And in every business or industry, you'll find that's the status most employers are looking for.

One thing's for sure. By not going through self-analysis of any kind, whether it be with this exercise or any other, including therapy, you will increase the likelihood of going down the same old path—the path you've taken in the past that led to the same dispiriting dead-end. The familiar refrains will go on and on.

I can't believe it, I'm laid off again!

That guy down the hall got the promotion I wanted!

I'm not getting anywhere in this place!

As Albert Einstein once observed, the definition of insanity is to keep doing the same thing over and over again and expecting a different result. If you keep getting caught up in one corporate downsizing after another, maybe it's time to look at why you are continually finding yourself in such a vulnerable position and to start rethinking your strategy so that history won't repeat itself.

For example, let me tell you about Don. He worked in the broadcasting division of a large multinational conglomerate and was laid off when his job disappeared in a corporate downsizing.

After a year of searching for another job, he was offered a position as copywriter at the same company's in-house corporate advertising department, and he took it. Within three years, this job too was eliminated in another downsizing.

What Don enjoyed was writing, and he had always harbored the dream of becoming an author and writing full-time. Rather than just take another job somewhere, he considered that perhaps now was the time to pursue his dream. But how could he support himself and his family while doing so?

He later explained to me that his former company had a reputation for taking the "neutron bomb" approach to cutting costs: the buildings would remain and the work would still have to be done but much of the workforce would be gone. So he contacted departments in the company, which still had copywriting needs and with whom he had had a prior relationship, and offered his services on a freelance basis. "They didn't have to pay me benefits or healthcare costs—those came out of my pocket—so it was much less expensive to hire me as a vendor than to put me on the payroll again, which appealed to the corporate bean counters," Don says. "And I could charge more per hour than I could ever have gotten as an employee and yet still remain more of a bargain than using an outside commercial agency. I got one assignment, which led to another and another. Freelancing sustained me for years while I wrote books on the side, until I was able to become a self-sustaining author of my own books plus the ghostwriter of many more in the 1990s."

Now retired, Don admits that it wasn't always easy being his own boss. "But I'm glad I took the shot after I was let go the second time," he says. "Knowing I couldn't be fired, passed over, downsized, or trapped again—that my fate was now entirely in my own hands—gave me the boost I needed to turn what seemed at the time like a setback into an advantage."

If an exercise in self-analysis and self-validation fails to lessen the depression you're in and convert it to motivation, seeking professional therapy might be beneficial in helping you turn the corner. As I've already noted, typically it's never one thing that will send you into an emotional tailspin in a job crisis, it's usually several things that come crashing down on you all at once.

When I was passed over for that promised promotion I told you about, I was also going through a divorce and dealing with a host of other difficulties. As I spiraled into depression, I sought therapy to help pull me out of it. It worked! Together with my own efforts at self-analysis and advice from friends and mentors, therapy got me feeling better about myself again so that I could start moving forward.

4. Convert Unfocused And Unproductive Behavior To Clarity And Purpose

Primary Objective: Hit the ground running by developing and maintaining your current circle of key employment contacts. Outline a general but clear plan of action to seek the job or career you want.

Combating this last saboteur is the final key to unlocking your ability to sell yourself, with the self-assurance of knowing you are going after the right job in the right field in the right way. Actually going after it is what you will take on in Chapter 4 where, among other things, you will learn how to craft an incisive pitch for the interviews you will be setting up. At this stage, however, you have no interviews to prepare for yet. Interviews are your goal, so you need to be focused and ready for action when the time comes. A recruiter will not put you out there for job consideration otherwise.

If you've done what's required to control or overcome the other saboteurs, you should have a much easier time tackling this one. That's because you will have already reached out to a mentor and resumed contact with former colleagues and friends. You will have listened to their insights, considered their feedback about you, and absorbed what you've learned so that you are now able to clearly see what's been holding you back or keeping you at a standstill in your job search.

In a calm, less defensive, and more open manner, you will have solicited pertinent advice from every appropriate quarter by asking the right questions, such as

- If you were me, how would you go about reaching out to other recruiters I haven't met before?

- Do I present a positive picture of myself to them and their clients?

- Have I repositioned myself so that the key players for the job I'm seeking will want to return my calls?

You will have been able to let go of your anger and desire to get even for being dismissed or for being passed over. Through validation by others and from regaining your own sense of self-worth, you will have found the desire to become an A-Plus performer, in whatever occupation you choose, and the motivation to get there. And through much self-reflection and soul-searching, you will now have a much sharper view of your occupational interests, skills, and goals. You will know the right field, the right job, and perhaps even the right company that will now fit you best rather than the other way around.

MEMO FROM SANDER

Brick and mortar recruiters versus online job-hunting sites-which is your best bet? Here's what Human Resources professionals tell me: "We have had some success with online recruiting; it's a good alternative (like online dating). It allows us to conduct searches 24/7 for candidates anywhere at minimal expense, and that's a big convenience. However, for specialized searches we would turn to brick and mortar recruiters because they are prepared to weed out the unqualified. That's their business, whereas with online recruiting, the initial screening is up to us, and as that's not our business, the process can be less efficient. The bottom line, though, is we are open to using both types of recruitment resources, depending upon the circumstances and our needs."

As a result of the exercises you've gone through and the actions you've already taken, you are now ready to put together a general action plan to prepare you to face the challenges I talk about in Chapter 4. This plan will ease you into a structured daily approach to get the ball rolling and to keep it moving steadily forward.

Sit down and start putting together a general outline of what you are going to do—and when—to move forward. This outline should be based on what you have now learned about your strengths and weaknesses, your key abilities and your value to prospects, your future job or change of career interests, and what's most important to you personally and professionally in terms of your goals for employment. Here is an example:

General Plan of Action

Week 1

Monday: Research types of positions in your selected field both online and with colleagues (people you have worked with in the past). Craft well-thought-out language for your résumé and interviews and seek out a good editor.

Tuesday: Begin researching job opportunities in your field online. Start to tell acquaintances of your search.

Wednesday: Continue researching job opportunities with colleagues and online. Start to inquire about job opportunities in everyday conversation with new acquaintances.

Thursday: Begin reconnecting with known recruiters/former employers for job leads in your selected field.

Friday: Continue reconnecting with leaders and known recruiters/former employers for potential job leads.

Don't bite off more than you can chew! It's easy to lose enthusiasm. Allow items to spill over to additional days or weeks if necessary. Tick off each item as it is accomplished. Once you're done, you will feel not only empowered but also emboldened to take on the job market, as you'll see in Chapter 4. You will be armed and ready to begin pursuit of the next new chapter in your life. And you can turn the page and begin that journey.

RECRUITER'S MEMO

"Tell everyone you know well or casually that you're looking for work. Do your homework checking the job boards, such as Indeed.com and the career/job pages of companies you're interested in working for. Look at your LinkedIn.com connections to see if you know anyone at those companies and ask for introductions. Explain that you're unemployed because of [reason] and would appreciate any introductions. After a career reversal, I truly believe that most people don't know what to do, so they resort to feeling bad for themselves or angry with their employers. When it is brought to their attention that this might not be the best use of their energy, most people realize that to be true and are able to become more productive."

Part II

"YOU'RE HIRED!"

Chapter 4

Successfully Sell Yourself...Even in a Jobless Economy!

*"Your premium brand had better be delivering something special,
or it's not going to get the business."*
-- Warren Buffett, American Entrepreneur and Investor

*"A brand for a company is like a reputation for a person. You earn
reputation by trying to do hard things well."*
-- Jeff Bezos, Amazon.com Founder

If your job has disappeared because of a merger, divestiture, downsizing, or whatever, what's your next move? Do you want to get back on exactly the same horse on the same merry-go-round or are you open to trying something different? If so, how different? And, if your job is on the line, what's your plan if it goes away?

Here is where you begin creating the next chapter of your life with a focused outcome-oriented strategy for achieving happiness and success in your next position. Here is where you will chart a plan to

- develop your unique, personal brand,

- reach out smartly to recruiters—especially niche recruiters—with a great elevator pitch and build a warm and productive relationship with them,

- create a killer résumé that emphasizes your strengths and accomplishments, not just your employment history (nobody cares!), and realistically prepare yourself for job interviews after many role plays with mentors,

- make the most of your references—particularly former bosses and Human Resources departments, and be certain they are all saying the same thing about why you left the company.

Here is where you will identify what's working for you now and might still stand improving; what's broken and fixable; and what isn't working and should be scrapped. You will learn what winners do to move forward with certainty, confidence, and success.

Develop Your Unique, Personal Brand

Seth was the managing director of a very profitable candy manufacturing company in the Midwest. He reported directly to the company's CEO, a position he hoped to move into one day. Seth's duties included sales and marketing of the company's products as well as managing operations in the plant where these products were made. But being a marketing innovator, Seth privately admitted, only to me and close friends, he got more of a kick out of his sales and marketing role, bringing the company's brand to number one in the marketplace, than he did in his operations role.

As a result, he sometimes didn't pay as close attention to some aspects of operations as he should have. Rather than spending time with his manufacturing people and cultivating relationships with them, he depended too much on the reports from his head of plant operations.

During one of the biannual FDA inspections, deficiencies in his company's manufacturing process were discovered that raised health concerns. If Seth had formed relationships, he might have gotten a heads-up from his manufacturing people; instead, he was blindsided. He had to shut down the plant immediately and pull a key product from the market. Four months later the quality control problems were corrected, and the plant was back on its feet and able to start manufacturing candy again.

A considerable amount of money was lost. That, coupled with the publicity nightmare the snafu had caused, made Seth face up to the cold hard fact that it was highly unlikely he would become CEO at that company or at any other. He offered his resignation and it was accepted.

I met with Seth over lunch a few weeks later when he was visiting New York. He was quite downhearted and said to me, "Maybe now's the time to spend more time with the wife and kids." To which I quickly responded jovially, "But perhaps they don't want to spend more time with you." He laughed and admitted I was probably right. But what should he do?

Encouraged after we had talked some more, Seth looked up other old friends and former business colleagues while he was in town, and through them, he got wind of an opportunity in Europe—in the sales and marketing division of a French engineering company. Engineering is, of course, an altogether different area than candy manufacturing, but the business objective was still the same: bring the brand to number one or two in its respective marketplace.

Relying on his proven skills as a marketing innovator, Seth became a partner and bought into the engineering company and, eighteen months later, took over as CEO, largely because of his sales and marketing expertise, his ability to build a company's brand by emphasizing a product's strengths, and his determination to grow a business quickly. Before long, the company's brand was number one throughout France and number two in Europe.

Not long after, he was approached by another engineering firm in Germany that wanted to push its industrial product brand to a higher position in the marketplace. Another sales and marketing challenge! Deciding to continue with the French company, he eagerly pursued a different challenge: to outperform his German rivals. Over the next several years, Seth succeeded in bringing the French firm's industrial brand to number one in sales in Europe and in South Africa as well. Eventually he purchased the company outright with some partners.

So what's the lesson to be learned from Seth's story? To quote a cliché, every cloud has a silver lining. Well, maybe. But I think the more potent message we should take away from Seth's experience is this: In the wake of a profound professional setback, he found his way back and into a better-than-ever position. How? By discovering what he truly liked doing most, by acknowledging that he was very good at it, and by emphasizing that strength above everything else. In much the same way that he emphasizes a product's strengths to make the company brand number one in its respective market, he emphasized his own strength.

And so Seth has forged an image of himself as the "King of the Brand Builders," whose role is to lead a team that quickly advances their company brand to number one. And the powerful theme of Seth's story—and of this book—is that successfully branding yourself—recognizing the need to and knowing how to—is the way to land the job you want.

MEMO FROM SANDER

Once they've lifted themselves out of the doldrums and are eager to tackle the job market, many people immediately think *Better start writing that résumé right away.* And they sit down and start scratching out lists of their past jobs, their respective responsibilities in those jobs, and their educational background to sum up their history. WHO CARES? That kind of profile could fit anybody; it doesn't sell you. But if you've gone through all the soul-searching needed to come up with your personal brand, which clearly distinguishes you from the pack, you'll be ready to do your résumé right. Dan Schawbel, author of *Me 2.0: Build a Powerful Brand to Achieve Career Success* says:

"1. Image management is how to shape perceptions by changing who you are on the outside. Personal Branding is how we market ourselves to others by revealing who we are on the inside.

2. A good brand conveys intrinsic value, expectation of performance, trust and reduced risk, and is predictable.

3. Branding means demonstrating and aggressively promoting what you're known for; taking your reputation to a higher level of awareness and publicity.

4. By branding yourself, you separate yourself from the crowd and create greater impact."

That's why personal branding always comes first.

Of course, if branding ourselves were easy, we'd all be doing it automatically and would all be roaring successes. But the truth is that most of us do a terrible job branding ourselves—especially in preparing to tackle the job market. And the reason for this is we've never been trained to ask similar questions about ourselves that we do about the products we sell or the services we offer.

What is it? What does it do? What's the benefit of using it? Why should someone choose it over someone else's offering? These are the key questions we ask about products or services before marketing them.

When considering employment, we should likewise ask ourselves: *Who am I? What have I accomplished? What's my biggest strength and how does it benefit me and others? Why should someone want what I have to offer?* And most importantly, *How do I clearly separate myself from the competition?*

This question-and-answer process builds self-branding. Your personal brand emerges from your answers to these questions—questions you will already have considered in Part I when assessing yourself emotionally and professionally in the wake of a career setback. As a result, you will be one step ahead when considering your answers.

RECRUITER'S MEMO

"What do I look for first in an individual's brand? When candidates walk me through their résumé, I listen carefully to their reasons for moving on to a new role/different company. For me positivity is the most important theme. I don't want to hear that they weren't treated well or that their problems were someone else's fault. I want to hear that they learned all they could and now want to move on to continue the learning process. For example, I had an entry-level candidate tell me that he had been the smartest one at his summer internship at a hedge fund. He explained that it was a very disappointing experience, however, because instead of learning, he was teaching. And sometimes he was asked to pick up the coffee in the morning. Then he proceeded to tell me about his expensive watch collection. Not a candidate I'd put forward! On the flip side, I interviewed a foreign-born candidate, who is working as an au pair for a family in exchange for room and board and a chance to learn the native language. And when I asked him what else he's been doing since finishing school, he said he is working in a bakery. When I asked him for recipes, he responded that he doesn't actually bake; he just comes in at night and cleans up. I asked how he likes doing that. He said he LOVES it. His employer always treats him well, and he feels it is an honor to make sure the place is spotless before everyone arrives in the morning. That's positive branding!"

A brand is more than just a reputation or a well-known and memorable name. It is a presence and a force.

A global branding consultancy company called Interbrand (a division of Omnicom Group) specializes in brand strategy, brand analytics, and brand valuation. It also keeps tabs on and ranks the top one hundred brands throughout the world on an annual basis based on criteria ranging from financial performance to the role the brand plays in influencing customer and/or client decisions.

Since releasing its first Global Brands report in 1999, Interbrand has ranked Coca-Cola as the number one brand worldwide because, in the words of Jez Frampton, Interbrand Global CEO, (from "Insights on Coca-Cola Topping Best Global Brands 2012 Rankings"), "Wherever one goes in the world, Coca-Cola is there. Its name is more universally recognized than any other across the globe...Coke's brand promise of fun, freedom, and refreshment resonates nearly everywhere...Its edgy campaigns continue to push boundaries, its global presence increases by the year, and Coca-Cola reinforces its values by linking entertainment, brand and positive messaging in the minds of millions, if not billions."

The only time the Coca-Cola brand waned was when the company's marketing director decided it was time to tamper with the formula and update the brand to the "New Coke." But nobody wanted that brand. They wanted the "old Coke"; the brand they liked and could depend on for taste, price, and availability. In the immediate wake of this marketing disaster, the company was smart enough not to continue flogging a dead brand but pulled "New Coke" from shelves as quickly as feasible and restored the brand by introducing (or reintroducing) "old Coke" as "Classic Coke" in full acknowledgment of its mistake.

Apple is a well-known and famous brand. In 2012, Interbrand ranked it number two worldwide, up from number eight in 2011. It is the cool technology brand that most people think about first when they consider purchasing reliable computers, tablets, and other electronic devices because it is the brand they trust the most in terms of innovation and delivering on its design and performance promises.

Can the same criteria be applied to branding an individual? As we've seen from Seth's story, the answer clearly is "Yes!"

As with any company or organization, product or service, the purpose of branding is to distinguish yourself from your competitors in the job market. Your goal is not to be seen as ordinary but as extraordinary in some strong and perceptible way.

You don't want to walk into the office of a recruiter or potential employer without knowing how to define what is new and different about yourself versus someone else. The person who can really distinguish himself or herself as a WINNER will get the job. So this is what you must think about before anything else when preparing to enter the employment marketplace. You want to be perceived as being as dependable as Coke. You want employers to clearly see when they bring you on board what's in it for them.

You must be prepared to communicate to the key people as concisely as possible what it is YOU bring to the party that no one else can, even if only a resounding enthusiasm for the job or an eagerness to be given the chance to prove yourself. And you must support your personal branding with facts, because they will be checked—for sure!

RECRUITER'S MEMO

"In an interview you may very well be asked, 'If we were to call your former boss and ask for an assessment of your greatest strengths and greatest weakness, what would he [or she] say?' You have to practice questions like that and be sure your responses will agree with those of your former boss, because we will check. For example, a solid response might go as follows: 'My biggest strength, I believe, is that I'm a tireless worker. I'm very focused and have managed to build every product I've launched into one of the top three performers at the company. As far as weaknesses are concerned, I suppose I don't show a lot of tact sometimes when people under me aren't on the same page. I can be very tough on them. This is a weakness you may hear about me.' That's smart branding—so long as it's accurate!"

Tell me how you are going to make my company or organization more productive.

Are you aware of some of the challenges the company is facing at the present?

Tell me your strategy for getting the best out of people. Our people are good people, but I know they can do better if properly motivated. How can you achieve that for the company?

These are among the many targeted and unspoken questions you are really being asked by employers and the recruiters they retain. And if you can answer them satisfactorily, then you've got a personal brand you can sell—one that may be able to get you a coveted position. What recruiters desire are candidates they can market to the client confidently. They are reluctant to take on anyone whose reasons for being out of work or seeking a better job are tough to explain. It's a chance, I'm told, they won't take.

Let's say your area of interest and expertise is in the technology sector—specifically software engineering and cyberspace design. You are having an interview with a recruiter or potential employer, not because you look good in a business suit or casual dress (though appearance can still be important), but because there is a need...say for a company research director.

The company wants someone who is not of the old school, but a new cool candidate, technology savvy, and Internet proficient. The company CEO wants the person selected to help persuade her reluctant board of directors to spend more money on information technology to bolster the company's competitive edge. The candidate for such a job, who has fully considered and knows his or her personal brand, might respond something like this:

"You're so right about the importance of web-based information as a commercial driver. Let me tell you about an innovative web-based product developed with some of my colleagues at my previous job. It's a website that eases the tension of people who will be driving into any major city—like Boston, New York, Chicago—for dinner and a show. Using this new site, they can locate a parking garage close to their restaurant or theater, book their parking spot in advance on the site, and pay a discounted fee. The response to this 'worry-free parking' convenience has been overwhelming."

Wow! thinks the interviewer. *This gal* [or guy] *really gets what we're about. I can't imagine why she* [he] *was let go. Attitude, work habits, what?*

As if reading the interviewer's thoughts, the candidate continues: "I was up for the next phase of researching and developing more new products and services like this, but the company brought in a new supervisor who preferred working with people on his team that he knew. He was more comfortable forming his own team, so several of us were let go. I was one of them."

This candidate's entire pitch—delivered in just a few minutes— tells the story and communicates the candidate's personal brand in clear, concise, compelling, employer-focused "what's in it for me" terms.

In the field of education, communicating your personal brand when seeking a new teaching job in the wake of across-the-board layoffs and school closings might go something like this:

"As I'm sure you're aware, many schools in the Brooklyn area are being closed because they're considered to be underachieving. My school was one of them. My students consistently did well, so neither they nor I were poor performers. In fact, I was consistently ranked quite high in my job performance by parents, the principal, and colleagues. But the school overall was judged as performing below standards and expectations and was closed. We faculty members all lost our jobs. But my credentials and performance reviews and references will speak for themselves."

You get the idea and the goal: to be seen as above average and dependable—that you too can be trusted to deliver satisfaction, just like that bottle or can of Classic Coke.

Reach Out Smartly to Recruiters

Companies, professional organizations, and nonprofits hire recruiters to find the right candidate to fill a specific job opening. Successful recruiters know clients will keep coming back for their employment needs, providing a steady stream of income. As positive word-of-mouth builds, recruiters will add more satisfied clients, strengthening their reputations and growing their incomes even more.

It follows then that successful recruiters will not jeopardize their position by taking just anybody who approaches them with a résumé—not even as a favor for a friend. Only the best—that's the branding recruiters seek to establish for themselves and want to maintain, because it's the ticket to ensure client confidence and loyalty.

MEMO FROM SANDER

If recruiters don't supply their clients with well-researched, top-shelf talent, the word will quickly get around not to use those recruiters anymore. That's why a recruiter is careful to take on only those individuals whose personal brand spells W-I-N-N-E-R. No others need apply for fear of damaging the recruiter's reputation in the marketplace.

By contrast, your local employment agency or temp service works on volume. They don't have the time or, usually, the tenacity to do the kind of screening and background checking that more specialized recruiters do. Nevertheless, this doesn't mean you cannot apply many of the same principles, tips, and techniques you've learned in this book to approaching them. Just because these volume recruiters fill entry and mid-level types of jobs doesn't mean you shouldn't give yourself an edge by developing a personal brand to pitch to them. A personal brand makes you stand out and be noticed; it separates you from the pack.

Whether you are reaching out to an exclusive, top-tier executive recruiter or to a high-volume, all-purpose employment agency, your goals are the same: to expand your circle of employment contacts and to be successful in your search for the best possible position that fits your aspirations.

MEMO FROM SANDER

Employee recruitment is not an amorphous, one-size-fits-all business. Recruiters who specialize in serving specific needs of businesses and institutions-whether public, private, or nonprofit-are called retained, or niche, recruiters. So after you have discovered your own niche, look for that niche recruiter. For a general list of niche recruiters nationwide and the fields they target, see the Resources section at the end of this book.

In Chapter 3, I discussed the importance of reaching out to old bosses, mentors, peers, family, friends, and recruiters you've used in the past as part of the healing process following a job setback.

It's a surefire method of recovering from the crisis of confidence you felt and reclaiming your self-esteem.

With that door now successfully open, the next step is to go through it and, having branded yourself, reach out to many of these same folks again—this time for new contacts and leads and to practice your new elevator pitch. The key here is to expand your reach in the job market and build new professional relationships, particularly with newly found niche recruiters.

MEMO FROM SANDER

Identify up front whether the recruiters you are speaking to are contingency or retained (niche) recruiters-this is a big deal. Contingency recruiters can send your résumé out to multiple employers, resulting in your losing control of who gets it and how many times. This practice breeds overmarketing of your résumé and seldom leads to a satisfactory opportunity. You can and should negotiate with contingency recruiters to limit their exposure of your résumé to agreed-on prospects. Retained recruiters are on a specific search and usually closer to the company retaining them, so be careful about saying anything disparaging or expressing doubts since this may eliminate you from consideration. Retained recruiters already have the job in hand, and hopefully, you will fit the job profile. If you are intensely interested in the job being described to you, take the profile descriptors and use them in your personal branding blurb wherever they fit. Let the recruiters help you to brand yourself.

It's as simple as this: the better your relationship with recruiters, the better your chances of success in the job search. If a recruiter believes in you (your brand) enough to try and market you, the harder that recruiter will sell on your behalf. It's just human nature: that all other things being equal—qualifications, accomplishments and so on—a recruiter will go to bat more for a candidate he or she has come to know, like, and have faith in than a remote, over-the-transom stranger.

So establishing empathy early on with all your contacts, especially recruiters new to you, as well as understanding human nature is the way to start over again in the job market with renewed vigor, passion, and determination.

RECRUITER'S MEMO

"Broadly defined, old confidants are centers of influence that can help you to expand your network. They include former bosses, peers, subordinates, former competitors, and industry and trade association contacts. Anyone professionally who can help you reach new decision makers should become your new BFF [best friend forever]."

If you know the business contact or recruiter from a past relationship, warm things up first by recalling some detail of that relationship. For example, "Bob, it's really good to hear your voice again after all this time. I was just thinking about you and the time when you were president of a direct mail firm. You were like the number one guy in your field back then when I was your client, and you sure mentored me. I've never forgotten that. Great memories! Well, Bob, here's my situation now. As you may know, my company had a major reorganization, and in that reorganization, my business unit was eliminated. So I'm out of work along with everybody else. I was hoping you could help me move on as you did in the past."

From there, you can get into asking about private recruiters or other leads "Bob" may be aware of, that you're not, to put you on the right road. You will have achieved this without appearing pushy or entitled. On the contrary, you will have reestablished a relationship that you have acknowledged meant much to you in the past, and still does. "Bob" is now in the position of wanting to help you. Whether he can, or not, at this particular time is another matter, which is why you will want to maintain contact and further develop the relationship by making "Bob" part of your ongoing network.

MEMO FROM SANDER

Apply the 20/80 rule when contacting new recruiters and employers. You talk twenty percent of the time and let them talk eighty percent of the time while you listen. They're busy people, and if you are successful in getting them on the phone, you've got about fifteen minutes to tell them how wonderful you are and what you can do for them. The questions you ask will also separate you from the competition, so consider them carefully before asking them. Make sure they're pertinent and add value to your overall branding pitch.

If business contacts or niche recruiters you've found are unknown to you, warming things up with a little relationship building early on is a good idea. You just need to do a little research on these individuals and their organization before contacting them. With a nod to Kevin Bacon, I call this the "six degrees of separation" strategy. Here's how it works.

There is always some connection—a person you may mutually know, a situation or place you may have shared—that you can make use of to establish an emotional connection early on and expand so the individual or organization will want to go to bat for you.

For example, the recruiter may have placed someone you once worked with or someone who worked for the same employer you did but at a different time. Go online and do a Google, Facebook, or LinkedIn search to find some commonality that will help you open the door. This search may turn out to reveal a connection that is extremely tenuous or one much closer and deeper than you would have believed or known about. But the likelihood is that you will find a connection, if you only look hard enough.

RECRUITER'S MEMO

"Don't ever send a query letter to a new contact that starts with 'Dear Recruiter:'. That is about as well received as mail at home addressed to 'Dear Occupant:'."

The degree to which you've cultivated and maintained your past business relationships can be a major selling point on your behalf that new recruiters and employers will take note of. It's a sign you might be able to bring some of those relationships along with you to your next employer—in the form of new clients or opportunities.

RECRUITER'S MEMO

"The best way to shut down relationships with recruiters is to negate their ability to present you. This means if you are going to entrust your résumé to a recruiter, don't send that résumé to all the companies the recruiter is likely to have in her arsenal. Make a choice. Either use your own networks and represent yourself, or trust your recruiter to give it her best shot for you first. The last thing you want to do is alienate your recruiter."

For example, suppose you are a well-known art director at a small advertising agency in a medium-sized market. You've won awards for your work from the local chamber of commerce and have received accolades at regional advertising competitions. Your clients love and praise you for the sales results and prestige your work has brought them. Your employer loves you too because happy clients are good for the agency.

However, you are often late for meetings or arrive late for work, and you've been criticized for this (even though you frequently work extra hours). In fact, your boss has cautioned you repeatedly about your lateness, but you think it's nothing serious. So you always dismiss the warnings. But your boss sees this behavior as a liability and now you've been put on notice in your performance reviews to "shape up or else."

It's the "or else" that has prompted you to start looking at other agencies for a better job, where the value you feel you offer will be more appreciated.

You are in the driver's seat here. Even though your persistent tardiness may be seen as a liability, you weren't hired for your ability to watch the clock. You were hired to make clients' brands shine, giving clients recognition and prestige. And you have done just that! When you present the combined package of your strengths and weaknesses to recruiters and potential employers, you should be candid about your habitual lateness. But, more importantly, your strengths are what count, and if a potential employer sees that you will consistently solve problems and please clients, he or she can work around your unusual schedule.

Business appreciates exceptional performance. That axiom is true not just in advertising but in every field—at small companies in minor markets, all the way up the ladder to huge companies in major markets. So, if you have received kudos—verbally, in e-mails, or in letters—from your current clients or from industry organizations, be sure to highlight your acknowledged accomplishments when speaking to your recruiter and employer leads.

Conversely, think about how to present your liabilities, particularly if you expect your job performance will be checked out. Think how you can counter a negative response to your liabilities. Can you say anything positive about them? No one is perfect, but you can show you have learned from mistakes and worked hard to improve. But be warned! Recruiters tend to view assertions of change with skepticism.

RECRUITER'S MEMO

"I recommend researching the companies in your target industries and making a note of the top relevant leaders. Also consider which association and industry events or conferences are useful. If you are comfortable contacting the hosting organizations of these events or conferences, offer to help. Your service might include serving as a speaker, panelist, and/or moderator. The objective is to expand your network, and getting to, or close to, the podium really can multiply your efforts. You also might write an article for a relevant industry publication or an online magazine, or you might comment on blogs, or you might start your own blog. Topics should be within your area of interest or expertise and should convincingly show your knowledge of the subject. This will help Internet researchers find you."

Create a Killer Résumé

As you begin to craft a résumé for submission to recruiters and potential employers, put yourself in the position of the person receiving it. In other words, put your focus on your audience and approach writing your résumé as if you were the author of a book you hope will become a best seller. You want your reader's reaction to be, "This person is a find! I've GOT to tell people about this gal!"

That reaction also describes the mind-set you need to be in when developing your résumé. It all comes down to communicating accomplishments and not a boring list of all the jobs you've had in the past. (Twenty years of work experience is more than enough to list.) Whether you're looking for a job as an engineer, IT person, writer, or salesperson; whether you're in your thirties or your fifties; whether you're just starting out or looking for a better job, I repeat: communicating value and accomplishments is the key to creating a killer résumé.

MEMO FROM SANDER

If you're in a mid-level position at a company that has given you the pink slip for whatever reason, chances are the company's Human Resources people may offer you outplacement services, where an outside firm that specializes in crafting résumés for professionals looking for work helps you with your résumé. Even if you're not offered outplacement services, you can still hire one of these firms on your own [see the Resources section], although this can be costly. Be aware though that recruiters and employers can easily spot an outplacement résumé-or a résumé crafted from one of the many books or websites on résumé writing because of the surplus of hyperbolic adjectives typically found in them. Do you believe such words as "highly motivated," "highly skilled," "successful leader" even begin to tell your story of how you are different from others? They don't. So do your best to remove all such adjectives from your résumé-surgically if necessary. It's all about your accomplishments.

The process of developing your personal brand, which you have already gone through, lays the foundation for the challenge you face here because now you are well versed in the value you can add to any organization. That's important to remember because your achievements—what you can do for your prospective employer—will land you the job, not your past employment history or previous duties.

For example, take the title "Director, Sales." It sounds

important. But it tells your résumé reader absolutely nothing about what you actually did for your employer that will make the reader sit up and take notice. Did you ever exceed your sales or production quota? Did an idea of yours spawn a new market or cause a client to positively comment? If yes, by how much and how often? Was your team ranked in the top five? By whom, for what? That's the kind of accomplishment detail that communicates value to the prospective employer.

Say you are a sales manager for a news magazine looking to increase circulation, and you have opened up a new demographic or a new geography. You helped enlarge readership or you managed to target affluent readers. What were the wins you brought in and what did they translate to in terms of revenues for the publisher? If you've got a story to tell here, then your ingenuity and understanding of the market will help to sell you.

If you were a key player in the development of a new product that became your former company's big seller or helped gain entrée to a new market, that's the added value you should be communicating (even if you weren't in on the sales end of things), because sales start with an innovative product or service idea, and that's where you come in.

What if you're in your early twenties, digitally adept and social-networking savvy; have already entered the workforce; and are looking for a better job in the exploding technology arena, yet you don't have a list of work accomplishments to date...now what?

Well, maybe you and your techno-geek buddies used to sit around brainstorming "making money" ideas in your dorm room. Maybe you and your posse have a system to swap clothes or find the most low-cost outlet-shopping deals. Your ideas to create new revenue streams or new marketing opportunities are points you can use on your résumé to tell your story and distinguish yourself and to advance your personal brand of "Innovator."

Perhaps you developed a unique study guide app or a new weight-loss app that everybody in your class soon began using on their smartphones or tablets, giving you a following. These are accomplishments you can use to communicate your value to IT product development/technology recruiters and potential employers, because they show that you possess the qualities of creativity, ingenuity, initiative, practical knowledge, marketing savvy, and success (even in nascent form) that are so widely valued in the work world.

RECRUITER'S MEMO

"I look for relevant work experience, including company names. It is important to me that a candidate is loyal—stays with an employer for a while and doesn't job-hop too much. I prefer a liberal arts degree to a business or technical degree. I believe liberal arts studies help people learn how to think and help create well-rounded individuals. Being part of a team or a club for multiple years also shows commitment and might demonstrate leadership."

In the leadership course I teach to MBAs at Fordham University Graduate School of Business Administration, creative brainstorming and real world problem solving is not only encouraged but is also the topic of the final exam. In the exam, the students are asked to define a challenge, to provide a solution for it in the form of a new product or service, and to create a full business plan to support the solution. Solutions to these challenges have even resulted in several students registering patents—definitely a plus on anybody's résumé.

In response to a problem about unsanitary public lavatories, for example, one team came up with the idea for a foot-operated toilet seat that lifts and closes with a press of the toe pedal, so that hands never have contact with the toilet except to flush it. (And in some public lavatories, flushing is already automated.) This solution provides a convenient, less messy, and more sanitary public toilet and may be adapted for private home use. The student team has since designed a prototype and is pursuing funding to develop the product and take it to market. Whether it succeeds or not is almost beside the point; the innovation itself is a proud achievement featured on each team member's résumé.

Another student came up with a solution in her exam for a product that has since been taken to market—a portable replacement heel usable on any high-heel shoe. If a heel should break off during work or on a date, all the wearer has to do is attach the portable one for a temporary fix—like putting a spare tire on a car following a blowout.

> **RECRUITER'S MEMO**
>
> "Candidates should stress their competency areas. They might even want to include them at the very top of their résumé—for example, 'PMP Certified,' 'Supply Chain Expert.' Candidates should try, as much as possible, to highlight the KEY responsibilities pointing to their achievements, but without including everything down to 'Responsible for locking the file cabinets at night.'"

As part of an advanced curriculum, community colleges are developing new classes that include innovation, project management certification, incubating ideas, and developing entrepreneurship in arenas where jobs are available. And if you continue your education at a four-year school or pursue a graduate degree, most colleges and universities have job placement programs that canvas alumni for contacts and leads on behalf of graduating students entering the workforce.

Whether new-to-the-job-market candidates with little or no employment history or veteran job seekers with a long employment history, recruiters advise all to come to interviews prepared with up to four brief one or two minute problem-action-result (PAR) stories. These stories should concisely illustrate a difficulty faced, the way the candidate fixed the problem, and the positive outcome it generated.

With smart crafting, you can incorporate into your résumé narratives that show your value and present real-life credentials, which in a person starting out are practically nonexistent. Recruiters and employers are always on the lookout for hot prospects who are achievers and innovators. Candidates who understand THAT know preparing PAR stories helps them in their interviews and in their résumés.

RECRUITER'S MEMO

"If you choose to use recruiters, make sure that the person receiving your résumé operates in and networks well in your field. A focused approach to a job search using recruiters requires you to keep excellent notes on who is authorized to submit your résumé and where. Your résumé should not leave their office unless you know where it's going and why."

Avoiding Pitfalls in Your Résumé

Sarah is a very sharp mid-level executive with a great ability to increase revenue and a great list of accomplishments she can point to in her career so far. But Sarah is a lone wolf who works better on her own. As a result, her relationship with her direct reports is a bit rocky. Sarah doesn't tolerate any slipups and criticizes her staff when they fail to live up to her expectations.

Eventually, Sarah was let go by her large multinational employer for that very reason.

Poor Sarah has since had no luck finding a comparable job at a similarly large company because her managerial reputation keeps following her, and potential employers don't want headaches. Recognizing all this, Sarah could say to recruiters that she has turned over a new leaf and tempered her managerial style, but as indicated earlier, recruiters tend to view such assertions of change with skepticism. For Sarah, this is a hurdle in her résumé that is just too high for her to overcome. So, what should she do?

I suggested to Sarah that she focus her job search on smaller entrepreneurial companies where the negatives in her managerial history may be considered less important than her accomplishments, because smaller companies looking to move up tend to be hungrier than larger companies. Since she's the kind of person who really needs to work by herself to do her best, using outside vendors when and if she needs them, a smaller company with less hierarchy to serve and fewer or no staff to manage might be a better fit for her.

Seeking bigger is not always better, especially if you've got a negative in your résumé like Sarah has. The main objective is always to sell yourself in the best possible way to the employer best able to let you shine—not to keep banging your head against an unyielding wall. So, Sarah has now started canvassing smaller companies and their recruiters, and she is shaping her résumé accordingly to demonstrate her core ability of jumping the magic revenue curve. What boss wouldn't want that skill?

RECRUITER'S MEMO

"A client lost his job on a trading desk at a Wall Street brokerage house. He decided to apply for a job at a competitor and took his rather large book of business to show them. He was told that they already do business with the companies on his list. He and I met and I asked him if they did business with the specific people on his list. The relationships are what they'd be buying when hiring him, not the company names, and he should emphasize that. He called them back, had that conversation, and was hired the following week."

Another pitfall in your résumé—one that affects many job seekers today, especially older ones—is insufficiently projecting your viability. Your résumé may lack any mention of new skill development. Either you have not kept up with new trends and developments in your field and can't add this point, or you have kept up but don't think to show it on your résumé. Either reason, not showing any skills can be a huge disadvantage to those entering or reentering the job market.

For example, if you're an art director who still uses a drawing board and Sharpie pens when most businesses today have gone almost entirely digital with their creative output, you've got a marketability problem that cannot be easily surmounted with excuses. This problem must be eliminated—and by that, I don't mean just taking an eraser to it on your résumé.

Take some courses at your local community college or business school in whatever area you need to bring yourself up to speed—for example, learn how to design on an Apple Mac computer using the latest design software and get good at it—before taking your revised résumé to market. Now you can point to your determination to stay current in the art direction field as part of your unique personal brand, along with listing your past accomplishments at the drawing board.

Recruiters and employers are inclined to look favorably on job candidates who do not carry on doing things the same old way when they can learn new ways to work more creatively, productively, cost-effectively—and who empower themselves to do so.

RECRUITER'S MEMO

"Don't market yourself with different résumés. Develop ONE résumé that accurately represents you and the value you offer. Remember, you are only one person."

Get Input from Colleagues

Once you've completed a draft of your killer résumé, give it to some of your closest colleagues and mentors to comment on. See if they judge it to be a "killer résumé." Pick just two or three for their input, not seven or eight; too much feedback may make you crazy. And don't tell them about each other. You don't want them comparing notes—nor do you want to risk putting anybody's nose out of joint because you didn't turn to them exclusively.

Be sure to tell them the kind of feedback you're looking for. For example:

Is my résumé too long or too short?

Am I focusing on the right things?

Would you hire me based on what you see in my résumé?

Above all, be sure to insist that they be honest with you and not hold back for fear of offending you. Be clear you want the unvarnished truth and won't take offense at anything they say. You want concrete, constructive criticism and suggestions that will help to sell you, so urge them to be blunt.

Building a Résumé

Here are two résumé examples, which show a killer résumé in two commonly used résumé formats.

Example 1, John Doe, shows the most common format: a chronological résumé. Laura Edwards, ExecSearches Résumé Reviewer, states this résumé presents work history (positions and accomplishments) in reverse chronological order and is best used by candidates who have steadily moved forward in their organization or career in no more than two different fields. The format "highlights growth and maturity" and is the one seen most often by recruiters and employers because it "provides an easy-to-follow structure for interviews." The chronological format is NOT good to use if you are changing careers or reentering the job market after a long absence.

Example 2, Jane Doe, is a functional résumé. Edwards explains that the functional format focuses on the candidate's skills and experience "rather than place of employment, which makes it ideal for mid-career changers or recent grads." The key to structuring a functional résumé when it is being used for a career change (or for entering the job market) is to identify the skills that are important in the new career. Those will be the section headings. The caution for this format is that "many employers are made immediately suspicious by these resumes since they are also often used to hide spotty employment records." So, have a colleague read your résumé and suggest the "suspicious" questions it may trigger. And practice your answers!

In the examples, notice that the sentences are short and easy to understand. The job descriptions and accomplishments read fast and make an impact. Remember that you do not need to go all the way back to your earliest job. A twenty to twenty-five year job history on a résumé is ample. And keep your resume to two pages, repeating your name and contact information on the second page. Force yourself not to be too lengthy. Good things DO come in small packages.

Example 1

JOHN DOE

Address

Phone   e-mail

DIGITAL MEDIA PROFESSIONAL

- Media Planning/Buying ~ Data Analysis ~ Campaign Management
- Hard working, dynamic, detail-oriented professional with over three successful years of client-facing agency experience
- Personable, passionate, critical thinker, presenter, and experienced manager
- Excellent analytical and communication skills; fast learner
- Proficient with Google Adwords, DFA (Doubleclick), Mediaplex, Invite Media, Commission Junction, Linkshare, comScore, Nielsen, Facebook, Twitter; exceptional with Excel and Powerpoint

PROFESSIONAL EXPERIENCE

Digital Media Supervisor: Company New York, NY
(2012-current)

- Manage digital media department: supervising, planning, buying, campaign management, and billing for multiple verticals, including travel (Client), consumer electronics (Client), skin care (Client), QSR (Client), and spirits (Client)

Account Manager: (Clients) New York, NY

(2010-2012)

- Managed multiple customers' expectations through weekly media performance presentations
- Served as a cross-functional conduit between agency departments and various clients
- Constructed and analyzed reports to provide deep data-based insights on a weekly basis
- Recognized need to overhaul display messaging to match search messaging which resulted in a dramatic and universal improvement in both click-through and conversion rates
- Coordinated the trafficking and reporting of complex campaigns containing thousands of placement lines using various reporting solutions
- Continually increased revenue by up-selling clients on fresh and impactful solutions

Media Planner: (Client) New York, NY

(2009-2010)

- Hit the ground running with minimal training and no prior marketing or online experience
- Planned, presented, and executed ad campaign within first month of being hired which has been renewed annually increasing revenue by $500,000
- Worked in team of three to strategize and plan multi-million dollar advertising campaigns
- Collaborated with publishers to create custom ad units and sponsorships that fit clients' needs
- Flourished in the fast-paced world of agency-side advertising requiring quick turnaround, effective communication, and time management

Guest Teacher: District 91 Idaho Falls, ID

(2006-2009)

- Designed and coordinated hands-on activities to enhance student interactions and critical thinking skills
- Evaluated each student's progress /adjusted teaching strategies for individual learning styles
- Planned individualized education-based programming for special needs students

EDUCATION

- Bachelor Degree: Political Science Major, Psychology Minor, College, City, State (2006)
- Advocate Training: Peer Counselor Seminar - Mediation and Relationship Counseling (2006)

Example 2

JANE DOE

Address

Phone   e-mail

SUMMARY

A quality-driven, detail-oriented professional with over thirty-years' business experience. Excellent editing, research, organizational, interpersonal, and leadership skills. Strong commitment to helping authors produce professional quality work that engenders pride and satisfaction, whether it is for family or the reading public. Mentor and advisor to friends and business associates on communication skills, both written and spoken.

PROFESSIONAL EXPERIENCE

WRITING

- Frequently recognized by management and coworkers for clear, effective communication.

- Developed and wrote easy-to-understand, clear training material to introduce a Change/Release Management system to business associates in different parts of the US.

- Wrote clear, uncomplicated directives and guidelines for Business Continuation planning and testing for an audience ranging from senior management to lower level associates.

- Redesigned business continuation training grids to effectively capture training skills in place and training skills needed.

- Developed and wrote extensive procedures for User Acceptance Testing of software systems.

- Provided clear, concise project summaries to

management including statuses, accomplishments, issues, and next steps.

- Wrote associate annual performance appraisals that accurately detailed accomplishments and areas for improvement.
- Created extensive and varied prototype scenarios to demonstrate a new imaging system.

EDITING / PROOFREADING

- Proofread and edited staff, project, and business associates' documentation for grammar, spelling, and accuracy before publication to division associates and management.
- Organized, managed, and edited documentation on critical Technology Division databases (Business Continuation, Program Packages, and Systems Implementation Documentation and Requests), used by the entire division to manage work.
- Edited requirements for a new Staff Business Continuation application written to replace labor-intensive manual activity.
- Edited associates' annual performance appraisals and individual development plans to ensure all requirements were met.

PROJECT MANAGEMENT

- Recognized for organizing to a deadline and handling multiple concurrent projects.
- Led team that developed requirements for an underwriting imaging system that replaced a labor-intensive manual system.
- Led team that developed requirements and implemented a Change/Release Management system that replaced a labor-intensive manual system.
- Coordinated Technology division's traditional and

pandemic business continuation planning and testing, collaborating with the Enterprise Business Continuation Office.

- Led team that provided multiple User Acceptance Test environments for regular monthly software releases. Enforced process and procedure to ensure test environments simulated production as much as possible and partnered successfully with business users, ensuring their satisfaction.
- Directed division's Y2K problem prevention activities and provided on-site trouble-shooting support 12/31/1999.

FREELANCE EDITING *(2010–Present)*

- Edited one historical novel, two short story collections, two memoirs, one poetry book, and one children's book.
- Proofread one memoir and one poetry book.
- Provided editing and proofreading advice for a novel and a memoir.

Company Business Technology Division

Director, Information Systems *(1999–2010)*

Manager, Information Systems *(1990–1999)*

Associate Systems Manager *(1984–1990)*

Programming Analyst *(1981–1984)*

Programmer *(1979–1981)*

EDUCATION

BA in Psychology, College, City, State
Graduate Study MBA (30 credits), College, City, State
Profession Certificate in Copyediting (2010) from
College, City, State

PROFESSIONAL DEVELOPMENT

FLMI (Fellow, Life Management Institute) Designation from
LOMA (Life Office Management Association)

COMMUNITY SERVICE

Rotary Club (1990–2000) City, State, Secretary 1995–2000
Kiwanis (2005–Present) City, State, Club Secretary, 2008–2011

Make the Most of Your References

Recruiters and employers do not look for character witnesses when they request a candidate's references. They look for confirmation of the candidate's claims. Does the picture of the candidate that emerges from the résumé mesh with the references' observations? Are the candidate's credits too good to be true? They will find out, I can assure you, because recruiters and employers put a great deal of emphasis on references—but only the right ones. Your Uncle Charlie or Aunt Millie or your friends, Robbie or Pam, just won't do.

In their haste to generate employment interviews, job seekers may not spend sufficient time considering the references they should offer. After a nanosecond of thought, they'll start scribbling reference names with little or no real consideration given to the best choices to tell the story they want told. In fact, most job applicants never even ask their references what they're going to say when the recruiter calls. That's like an attorney putting a witness on the stand whose testimony he's never heard before. It's a BIG no-no.

Recruiters especially, and employers too, put the most stock in the following tiers of references:

- Tier 1: Your immediate supervisor, former boss, or a board member (current or former).

- Tier 2: Peers (colleagues) at the same level who have worked with you in the past.

- Tier 3: Office manager or Human Resources—here's where that letter confirming the nature of your dismissal or departure (see Chapter 3) comes in.

- Tier 4: Subordinates—anyone who has worked under you in the past.

If they don't see all four tiers represented in the list of references you provide, be warned: recruiters or potential employers will surely do some digging and contact those folks on their own. So, the first step in making the most of your references is to consider your choices with great care and to be sure all four tiers are represented. If you don't have all four tiers—for example, an office manager or Human Resources reference—make sure, in your interview, you offer a valid reason why this reference is missing.

The next step is to make sure ahead of time (that means before you're asked for them) that your references are on the same page you are when they're contacted. This requires that you actually ask your references up front what they're going to say. You're not trying to put words in their mouth—you're just assessing whether their words will conform to what you say on the résumé. If not, at least you'll know before they are contacted, and then you can get someone else to be a reference. Or you can remind your forgetful reference of what you did together, if you feel he or she will support you in your job search.

It's all about being sure, in advance, that you have considered your references thoughtfully, strategically, and with sufficient follow-up; all of which takes time. You don't want to ask someone to be a reference for you, just say thanks if she says "Sure," and leave it at that. References are another tool in your arsenal to sell you, so give them the focus they deserve.

The third and final step to making the most of your references is not to include them in your résumé when you make initial contact with recruiters and employers. Always say: "References provided upon request." Often references are not mentioned or asked for in mid-level job searches. If yours are solid, add the line to your résumé. It says you have excellent credentials.

The reason for not including references is this: You want to hold on to this important selling tool until it's asked for. Recruiters and employers will only ask for references from those candidates they are considering most seriously. So, why waste their time, your time, and your references' time until you have reached that stage? Focus on getting to the subsequent interviews' stage first. Until then, keep your references under wraps.

Make the Most of Your Interview

The interview is when you finally make the most of all your prep work to sell yourself. And it's a two-way conversation!

James Caan, the well-known UK entrepreneur, highlights this in his blog post "The 3 Questions People Always Forget to Ask in an Interview." I've already stressed how important preparation is and Caan does too, but he goes one step further by providing three questions YOU should ask a prospective employer, if the circumstances fit.

"What qualities are you looking for in the person you are hoping to appoint?"

This question zeroes right in on the skills and experience the employer needs and gives you the opportunity to demonstrate you have what he or she is looking for.

"What scope is there for personal development at your company?"

This is a question that shows the interviewer that you are ambitious and looking to advance your career.

"Is there anything you have seen in the other people on the shortlist that you have not seen in me?"

A great closing question, it is still a risky one because you must be prepared for an honest answer. The answer will provide you with solid feedback that will identify where you need to improve and also give you a way to assess how well the interview went.

Sander's "Musts" To Successfully Sell Yourself

1. Define who you are—and what you can offer—by creating your own, unique personal brand.

2. Reach out as soon as you can to colleagues and recruiters for new leads and contacts, so you'll be ready to move forward. Maintain a continuing dialogue with them without becoming a nuisance.

3. Get an official termination letter from your former employer or Human Resources department that backs your explanation for leaving. Your former employer or Human Resources must support what you say in interviews with recruiters and future employers. This is critical!

4. Create a brilliant résumé and list of references you trust! Rehearse those references on the key points you will be making to potential new employers.

5. Role-play a detailed mock interview, including PAR stories, with close senior level business associates, recruiters, or Human Resources people with whom you've maintained a good relationship.

6. Research one or two of the potential employer's challenges and develop a few innovative ideas you can discreetly articulate during the interview.

7. Focus on what you can do for recruiters and potential employers during all your conversations—both formal and informal—with them. It's not about you; it's about them.

8. Create an interview aura that is warm and conversational. Speak sincerely and be you at your positive best.

9. Look smart: hair styled, shoes shined. Maintain good eye contact, smile, sit back in the chair with ankles crossed, and maintain your best Bill Clinton or Julia Roberts "listening smile" during the interview.

10. Ask insightful questions.

11. Adhere to the 20/80 rule—you speak twenty percent of the time and the interviewer speaks eighty percent.

12. Always wait until the interviewer finishes the question or comment before responding.

13. Ask the recruiter or employer (using "please") to feel free to speak to people with whom you have worked or who have worked for you and will support what you have said during the interview.

14. Write the recruiter or employer a note after the interview thanking the individual for the opportunity to present your case. Be sure the note is HANDWRITTEN—no e-mailed "Thank you."

15. If you don't get the job, ask the recruiter or employer's Human Resources department why not. More knowledge adds more power to your next attempt. Let them know that you recognize that.

"On one hand a wild emotional outburst might be a great motivational tactic and the sign of a real leader. On the other hand it's not good to trash your desk on your first day."

Chapter 5

Secure the Future...Your First Hundred Days on the Job!

"The credit belongs to the man who is actually in the arena, whose face is marred by dust and sweat and blood...who at the worst, if he fails, at least fails while daring greatly..."
Address at the Sorbonne, France, 1910
"Far better it is to dare mighty things, to win glorious triumphs, even though checkered by failure, than to take rank with those poor spirits who neither enjoy much nor suffer much, because they live in the gray twilight that knows not victory nor defeat."
Speech before the Hamilton Club, Chicago, 1899
-- Theodore Roosevelt (1858-1919), 26th President of the United States

In 1988, I was recruited by the Robert A. Becker Advertising Agency to be CEO. The agency was then on a downward trend and needed someone to help turn things around quickly with clients, such as Pfizer, Bristol-Myers Squibb (BMS), Merck, and Sandoz (now Novartis). I got the job, in large part, because I already had a relationship with many of these companies. What neither I nor the company that recruited me knew at the time, however, was the depth of the company's business downturn, which is not surprising because that sort of insider information is seldom broadcast. I found out soon enough though.

Just starting in my new position, I received a phone call from the marketing vice president at Merck, who had once worked for me during my Lederle days. He said to me, "Sander, why did you go over there? We're about to fire Becker." Knowing nothing of this, I was dumbstruck.

"Here's the story," he went on. "They handled our biggest product and blew it. I can't believe you went there. Why didn't you call me first?"

I had been made aware that Pfizer was already on its way out as a client, and now Merck too? In fact, by the time I came on board, every client they had, with the exception of Bristol-Myers Squibb, was gone or on the verge of going, taking sixty to seventy percent of the agency's business with them. And I soon learned that even Bristol-Myers Squibb was threatening to leave the agency! Under the circumstances, I suppose the logical decision would have been for me to quit. "You sold me a sack of lemons and so I'm heading for the door." Don't think it didn't occur to me. But there was another part of me that liked a big challenge, and turning around Becker's pharmaceutical fortunes certainly qualified.

Over the Thanksgiving weekend, I met with the Board of Directors of WCRS, the parent company that owned Becker, in London. The members were in a panic. "The shareholders will be all over us if you can't stop the hemorrhaging," they said to me. I knew what that meant. If I failed, I was toast and would be carrying that scorch with me wherever I searched for another job. Nevertheless, eyes open, I accepted the challenge and began to tackle it head-on.

There wasn't a lot I could do about the clients who had already left, but I could still go all-out to hold onto Bristol-Myers Squibb. That was the immediate objective to which I committed myself and my team. At the time, BMS had marketing troubles with the anti-anxiety drug BuSpar it had developed to compete with Valium and Ativan. Since this client was considering dropping us, they weren't inclined to share with us their whole BuSpar situation, so I spent some money (money we didn't have) and conducted my own market research to learn the issues involved.

The big clinical issue was that BuSpar took three weeks to show results, while Valium and Ativan kicked in within a week of taking them. So the crux of the marketing question was this: given that all three drugs were quality products but two of them worked faster, how could we persuade consumers to choose BuSpar over the others when they had to stick with it longer?

The answer was that BuSpar didn't produce the side effects of drowsiness and dizziness, like the other anti-anxiety competition did. Even though you had to stay on BuSpar longer for it to take effect, you would still be able to drive your car safely and function normally without worrying about feeling sleepy or dizzy.

Three months after taking over as Becker's CEO, I met with the senior people at BMS, who had agreed to give us a hearing "one last time." I laid out for them a campaign that would positively differentiate BuSpar from the other drugs, so that physicians would prescribe it and consumers would want to stick with it. They were impressed with the efforts we had made on our own to grasp the problem, and they loved the Big Idea solution we came up with. As a result, they gave us the go-ahead to develop and launch the new campaign. BuSpar sales exceeded quota that year by twenty-five percent!

Becker was losing a million dollars a month in revenue when I took over, and within eighteen months, we were back in the black making money. Our UK parent company boasted so much about this turnaround that a French media company called Euro RSCG made an offer to buy WCRS. The parent company accepted, and soon I was working for the French as CEO of a new agency called Euro RSCG Becker. And by the end of my fifteen-year tenure, we grew to number two in health care in the United States.

I'm sharing this story with you, not for any kudos, but because the points it makes go straight to the heart of this chapter.

Though it took eighteen months to bring the agency back into the black, the process to get us there began on day one by focusing on an early and achievable big win. ₌

Taking a year or more to complete a critical task in a new job and thus prove yourself to the boss used to be acceptable. But today's world demands faster action; proving yourself in a significant way should now take no more than one hundred days. And so, in this final chapter, I will discuss how to exceed expectations during the one-hundred-day period after you are hired or promoted, using techniques that can be applied over and over again and be successful for you every time.

Why one hundred days? Because it's just a tad over three months, which is short enough to create a true sense of urgency but also long enough to make significant achievement possible. The 100 Day Plan you develop is not to be taken lightly; it's like army boot camp, except that you'll be your own drill instructor. I still remember that constant bark from my army days: "Attention to detail, attention to detail!"

There are a variety of ways to achieve success—ways that build momentum early in the employer-employee relationship and that can be constructed around goals that are easily within reach (that is, go for the low-hanging fruit). Early wins whet your boss's appetite for more and starts to build the bond of trust you will need to meet your longer-term goals.

And, please note, you can't afford to wait for the job to begin before getting to work! From performing due diligence (Chapter 4) well before you even join the organization, you, as a new hire, already know what your longer-term goals are and that your first initiatives will be directed toward them. By developing an outcome-oriented plan that concentrates your time and energy on the key tasks that will bring you early wins, you'll be better able to focus and stick to your plan and handle the inevitable curveballs that will come at you. Like an old boss of mine used to say, "Want to know the formula for success? Plan the work. Work the plan."

Remember two key points: First, your new boss, as well as her or his Human Resources people, is looking at you to confirm she or he made the right choice. Your boss will react if you don't perform rapidly and reliably—in other words, if you don't meet, and even exceed, their expectations. And second, it's always about making the boss look good...always!

This is true at every level of employment—in every business, educational institution, research facility, or nonprofit organization. In building your career, you have got to excel at each job and beat out your competitors early on. And to excel, you've got to hit the ground hard and fast in your best running shoes.

Here are the steps to take to demonstrate your value to everyone in your first one hundred days:

1. *Notch up an early win.* Prioritize and put into action new ideas for achieving maximum results on a product or service in your first one hundred days on the job.

2. *Encourage and win buy-in from your key players:* your superiors, your team, and anyone who will play a role in your plan.

3. *Concentrate on a defined outcome:* the big win you want as a consequence of the actions you take, pushing the deadline back, if necessary.

4. *Keep your foot on the accelerator.* Maintain a non-stop focus on your to-do list. The days of multitasking are over; deal with the toughest issue first.

5. *Learn and teach those around you to embrace change.* It's tough, but don't recoil from change.

6. *Leave your mark* visibly and often. Keep moving forward. A little benign paranoia—keeping alert and knowing that you're the target of competitors—is a good trait for developing a leadership mindset.

Now let's take a closer look at each of these steps to success.

1. Notch Up an Early Win

When the General Motors Board of Directors ousted Fritz Henderson from his new job as Chief Executive Officer in 2009, he had been on the job just eight months. But it took no more time than that for GM's board to judge and dismiss Henderson—whose experience is not uncommon. Ron Johnson of J.C. Penney, same story, but he lasted about eighteen months.

Just as the pressures of an economic downturn force companies to make many more quick cuts in spending, they also lead to a lot more early beheadings, not just among chief executives but among all employee ranks. The research verifies that the turnover rate for chief executives who don't produce results tends to double in bad times, according to Stanford University Business School's Dirk Jenter. The lesson you should be taking away from this is that, as a new hire (in whatever capacity), you are vulnerable. This presents you with a huge challenge—but also with a great opportunity. Be smart in how you go about seizing that challenge, so that you can notch up that early big win.

Let's say you have just come on board as the new research director for a high-tech company that manufactures software. While pursuing the job, you have learned through your due diligence that the company has not launched a new product for years (hence the departure of the previous director). You have been hired specifically to reinvigorate that creative effort. What should you do in your new role to securely establish your personal brand as innovator right away? Score a solid win with a Big Idea that is achievable in the short term! As soon as your feet hit the floor on the morning of your first day at work, focus on what you can do within your first one hundred days to get that visible early win.

If, for example, you work in the marketing, product development, or research area of a company with one product line that's not doing well, but that product line could be combined with another that is doing much better, make the suggestion to form a new brand from the combination of the two. Awesome! You've got a road map for achieving that early win for yourself and for the company. Or if you're in a management position and you've got a product that's performing below quota, give it to your A-Plus sales representatives with a promise of a handsome bonus if they can hit one hundred percent of quota within the one-hundred-day time frame. It's a sure way to achieve that sought-after win and make you look like the new company star.

Always set your sights first on the low-hanging fruit—the target within easiest reach for scoring an early victory on your performance review. No matter what field you're in, this objective is a MUST! Right away you want to establish your bona fides— your personal brand as an A-Plus performer. So take the route of least struggle.

In the case of Becker, I focused on finding a way to retain Bristol-Myers Squibb as the lowest-hanging fruit, because this objective was much more achievable within one hundred days than bringing in new clients or winning back ones that had already left us. Those were longer-range objectives. However tenuously, Bristol-Myers Squibb was still with us—a bird in the hand. All I had to do was keep it from flying away.

MEMO FROM SANDER

Lew Platt, former CEO at Hewlett-Packard, has observed that success at any job can be a matter of just picking the right battle from the start. If you can find a few things that are noticeable flaws in your organization or department and fix them quickly, you can demonstrate your value and begin to secure your future very fast. So, always go first after the lowest-hanging fruit: something you know you can win to establish your personal brand and your credibility within the organization early on.

Let's look at another example of low-hanging fruit.

You are a journalist and you've just come on board at the *Wall Street Journal*, which, like most newspapers and magazines these days, is maintaining a staff that is lean and mean. You want to prove what a valuable asset you are and secure your future, so you aim to knock your bosses' socks off with something spectacular right away. How about some deep investigative reporting to unearth a story to rattle the cage of the banking industry?

That's a great idea (though perhaps not for the *Wall Street Journal*), but it's hardly low-hanging fruit. However, you have just heard that General Electric CEO Jeffrey Immelt has been named to head President Barack Obama's Council of Business Leaders on job creation. So you're quickly on the phone to arrange an interview with Mr. Immelt about the Council's goals and plans. They want the press, and you're the channel for their news— great, ripe, low-hanging fruit!

Maybe the local newspaper, not a big-time publication, has hired you to cover the regional business news, what do you do then?

Think about the trends in the business world: women opening businesses at a faster rate than men, entrepreneurs sprouting fast from the young millennial generation. Surely there is an interesting, comparable interview you could quickly land on the local level that parallels what is going on in the bigger business arena. The low-hanging fruit you choose is a matter of scale, depending upon your field, your job, and your market. Your objective in the end is all about making your boss (and the company) say, "The best thing I ever did was hiring her."

Here's another real-life example of notching up an early win with low-hanging fruit. When Procter & Gamble first introduced its top-selling detergent Tide into the Latin American market, sales were dismal, although there was clearly a want and a need for the product. Why the contradiction?

A very smart marketing director sized up the problem this way: Most people in these countries live below or slightly above the poverty level, so for them a big box of Tide is an expensive luxury. Nevertheless, they still want clean clothes as well as the feeling they have a touch of what well-to-do families have. This marketing director said, "Why don't we put Tide into small, affordable packets good for two washes that only cost five cents?" That's exactly what P&G did and Latin American sales of Tide skyrocketed.

Another way of notching up an early win is to consider what your boss may have told you (or what you discovered in your own research) that is keeping him or her tossing and turning at night—a business problem that needs immediate fixing.

Say you're a sales rep who's just been hired by an over-the-counter healthcare products manufacturer that has launched a new sleep aid. The sleep aid is missing quota, and your boss's stomach is eating holes in itself at night. You've got a clear go-ahead to notch up an early win for her—provided, of course, you can come up with a Big Idea solution to address the problem and fix it.

So, you put on your thinking cap. Your research has revealed, according to U.S. Department of Veterans Affairs' reports, that many veterans coming back from Iraq and Afghanistan are experiencing post-traumatic stress disorder (PTSD), a symptom of which is insomnia. What if your company were to give out the new sleep aid absolutely free to VA hospital pharmacies across the country for treating these returning vets? The only condition would be that your company is permitted to promote the donation of the drug—and its successful use by vets—in its advertising and marketing to nationwide drugstore chains such as Walgreens and CVS.

This Big Idea can take very little time to put into motion and yet can yield big returns very quickly. What drugstore chain or consumer with sleep issues would not want to purchase such a beneficial product? A sleep aid that successfully treats the recurring problems of insomnia from a company that first supplied it to our suffering veterans! Your boss will name you MVP for achieving such an all-around win-win for everybody—you, your boss, the company, the thousands of returning vets who are getting the drug for free, the consumers who are buying it from a sense of patriotic duty (and because it works for them too), and the drugstore chains who can't keep their shelves stocked fast enough!

2. Encourage and Win Buy-in from Your Key Players

The next component of your 100 Day Plan is to secure the necessary buy-in to go after the low-hanging fruit from your boss and any key players, so that they too share in your achievement.

Here's the secret: you have got to make your Big Idea seem

like it's theirs, not yours. This is a key strategy for securing your future that many employees overlook—mostly because they don't know how to share their accomplishments. They've never been taught sharing with others is critical to their own and their group's success. Think of the well-known acronym WIIFM or "What's in it for me?" When your key players look at your work and hear your ideas, they are thinking WIIFM every time.

Let's use our fictitious *Wall Street Journal* newbie to illustrate how encouraging buy-in from direct reports and/or from peers is an important ingredient in pulling off that early win-win. She hears about the Immelt appointment and goes straight into her managing editor's office and says, "Hey, boss, remember that conversation from about a week ago about GE's Jeff Immelt— you know, the one about how nobody has been able to get him to really open up in an interview about the economy for a really long time? Well, look at this new role he's been given by the president. I'll bet he'll open up about that. You've given me a great idea and I'd like to run with it. What do you say?" What do you think her boss will say? "By all means, give it a shot!"

This is why it's called buy-in: it's important currency for getting key people completely on board with your Big Idea. You make your idea a win-win by creating the impression that the idea started with them. You are simply executing it. And when successfully executed, you will have made them look good too.

Now here's the twist. The conversation our reporter reminded her boss about may actually have taken place in a different context. Doesn't matter. The point is to use a casual conversation, a telephone call, a note from management you saw on the company bulletin board, or a memo everybody's received from on high—something legit-sounding—to give substance and roots to whatever triggered your Big Idea, which you would now like your boss's OK to pursue.

If you'll recall my earlier hypothetical story about the Big Idea for boosting lagging sales of a new sleep aid product by offering it free to VA hospitals treating insomniac soldiers with PTSD, here's how that buy-in might have been encouraged.

You have heard the boss expressing anguish over the drug's poor sales: "We're getting killed here. We're only at eighty percent to quota! Can't be twenty percent down on our forecast!" After thinking the problem over and coming up with your Big Idea, you go to your boss and say, "I've done some research on the sleep aid sales issue that you're concerned about, and I think I have an approach that just might start rapidly increasing our market share, and get it done quickly. Your thoughts?" Chances are those thoughts will be *Go for it!*

Articles and books about getting ahead often discuss how important encouraging and winning buy-in from key people is to a successful career in any profession. But practical methods, like those I've described, are seldom given much detail, though they are widely practiced today by many successful business leaders to win buy-in for their ideas from their own superiors and boards of directors. Adopt and adapt these methods to your own situation and needs, and make it your priority to get buy-in from all key players above, below, and around you. It's the fuel for your successful 100 Day Plan—and beyond. Remember your key players: it's all about WIIFM!

3. Concentrate on a Defined Outcome

You're probably familiar with the question "Do you want it Tuesday or good?" It refers to the age-old debate about which is more important: should work be done on time or done well? The answer is both. But in this era of increasing global competition, continually turning out a higher-quality product or service than your competitor is more of a catalyst to growth, success, and job security than meeting arbitrary deadlines. If you have to choose between good or Tuesday, it's always better to be late with well-thought-out quality solutions than be on time with an average outcome.

This is not to say, of course, that deadlines are unimportant; they are a critical tool for getting everybody focused on the specific task or objective at hand. But in the end it's not the deadline that counts but the outcome. So, beginning day one on the job, keep your eye trained more on outcomes than deadlines—and that includes your own one-hundred-day deadline for exceeding expectations. No one is going to fire you for exceeding those expectations on day 110 or day 120. Exceeding expectations doesn't get people fired, demoted, or downsized. Failing to meet expectations does.

MEMO FROM SANDER

Persistence is critical to an outcome-oriented attitude. You must be willing to move past personal limitations to do whatever it takes to get the job done. It's necessary to quiet your anxieties and see a problem simply as territory you must navigate. Do not add an extra burden to an already tough situation by indulging your frustrations. Do not offer excuses or lay blame on others. Simply evaluate the best course of action, stay focused, and move forward to achieve your outcome.

OK, so you have selected the lowest-hanging fruit to go after for the quick win-win. You've established a sense of urgency and gotten the buy-in to go full speed ahead. Now you've got to concentrate on the specific result and work tirelessly toward achieving it.

This means getting your immediate boss to buy into eliminating any activities in the organization's tactical plan that do not relate to achieving that result. For example, it's not uncommon for many businesses to let their advertising agencies contribute to, or write, the company's tactical plan. As a consequence, recommendations can get into the plan that have little or no positive impact on specific strategic goals.

Because most advertising agencies are interested in making as much money as they possibly can, they may include activities that they believe are beneficial, but contribute nothing to achieving your anticipated outcome. An example is recommending expensive, high-quality, multi-page, multi-color visual aids for sales reps to market your product or service in an age where most customers get their product information directly online or from a sales rep's iPad demo. Fewer and fewer organizations create hard-copy brochures, but agencies continue recommending such tools because they make money producing them.

If you find one of your vendors' recommendations doesn't relate to meeting your outcome, it's dead weight; you should urge getting rid of it. You want to spend your time, your budget, and your resources only on what will get you the biggest return on investment for your outcome outlay.

What exactly do I mean by "outcome"? Let's say you work for Poland Springs and what keeps your boss up late at night is that Diet Coke is whipping your vitamin-based, bottled-water product in the marketplace. "What can we do? Give me a big idea!" is her or his explicit or implicit charge to you.

The Big Idea you come up with is your outcome, and your best game plan is to achieve it in one hundred days. Your outcome might be, "I'm going into the Diet Coke marketplace and introduce a brand new campaign to convert ten percent of all Diet

Coke drinkers to Poland Springs Vitamin Water" or "I'm going into a market where there is no specific preference for Diet Coke and put new vending machines with our drinks in every corporate building—until we own that market one hundred percent!" Then you focus on your outcome and work backward, chunking steps down into smaller outcomes that must be achieved here, here, and here in order to reach your ultimate outcome in one hundred days.

If by the one-hundred-day mark, you're only at an eight percent increase in sales, you can justifiably say to your boss: "You know, we're really moving in the right direction; we've managed an eight percent jump in sales that no one thought we could achieve. I need another twenty days to get the other two percent I promised." Neither your boss nor anyone else in the hierarchy will quibble, because in the end, it's the outcome that matters.

Adapt an outcome-oriented focus to your daily work life and you cross into the winner's box. Maybe you're just one of the hands working tirelessly for the end goal and not the one defining the ultimate outcome or the way to get there. For you, it's important to develop a personal outcome-oriented strategy: what you will deliver for your team at various stages during these first one hundred days to achieve the expected outcome. That's how to secure your future and be known as a team player. The key here is to rewrite your "Things To Do List" daily, reassessing your priorities and choosing your number one action to do TODAY.

4. Keep Your Foot on the Accelerator

MEMO FROM SANDER

After you have established your defined outcome, raise the bar! Of course, this means that, to succeed, you're now going to have to work even harder than you had originally planned. A true 100 Day Plan is not to be taken casually; it's something you'll want to create for every big project or new assignment you begin. It's the dividing line between good and great-your bosses will notice.

We spend nearly half of our waking hours thinking about something other than what we are doing in the present moment observe Harvard psychologists Matthew A. Killingsworth and Daniel T. Gilbert.

To come up with their conclusion, these researchers used an iPhone app they created to poll 2,250 subjects, ranging in age from 18 to 88, at random times throughout the day, asking them about what they were currently doing, how happy they were feeling, and whether or not they were thinking about their current activity or something else that was pleasant, unpleasant, or neutral. Subjects chose from twenty-two general activities and reported back that their minds wandered on average 46.9% of the time, and no less than 30% of the time during any given activity, except making love.

The researchers explain that mind wandering is an excellent predictor of people's happiness (and productivity). In fact, how often our minds leave the present and where they tend to go is a better predictor of our happiness than the activities in which we are engaged, they say. Their results appeared in the November 2010 issue of *Science*. "A human mind is a wandering mind, and a wandering mind is an unhappy mind," Killingsworth and Gilbert concluded. "The ability to think about what is not happening is a cognitive achievement that comes at an emotional cost." And that cost can often be our jobs—or our ability to get a job.

This statistical confirmation that our minds do indeed wander and that it is not necessarily a happy occurrence underscores the necessity of practicing the art of remaining focused. I say "practice" because staying focused takes a conscious effort. It requires us, particularly at work, to notice when our mind has gone somewhere else and to bring ourselves gently back to the moment. We must train ourselves to return from detours—to the present, past, or future—to the immediate task at hand. Because to be effective, one's mind must be centered and attentive.

Given the mind's natural tendencies to wander—thinking about what isn't happening or contemplating what used to happen, may happen, or has never happened—being centered and attentive is hard enough. But add a handheld device that takes us out of the present moment multiple times an hour and you can easily spend a day mentally elsewhere, without ever settling into the work in front of you. The smartphone, which is capable of connecting us to everything except the activity or person right in front of us, is making us even more distracted and dysfunctional. The gadget plays into our basic instinct to interrupt ourselves and to exit out of the present. How "smart" is that?

I recently worked with a group where one of the members confided that he puts his iPhone outside the shower so that he can hear the device while showering. Many people I spoke to said they felt their phones were controlling them, rather than the other way around. Others confessed that their smartphones and other devices make their workday feel like an ongoing, unending information deluge. "It's like our work lives are always in the 'on' mode," said one executive.

Do our smartphones create our wandering minds? Or do we possess a wandering mind that our smartphones support and encourage? The latter, I believe! Responding to a smartphone's constant interruption is easier than staying clearly focused on the task in front of us. So what should we do?

First, we have to acknowledge the natural tendency of the mind to want to escape the present moment at least half of the time. Simply accept this reality and commit to working with and through it.

Second, we must identify when we feel the most productive and the happiest at work. This is the "in the zone" high that makes work enjoyable. Simultaneously, we have to acknowledge how the smartphone-in-the-pocket syndrome impedes heightened productivity.

And third, we have to ask ourselves every day, "Am I ready to stop limiting my success by having my interrupters turned on all the time? How important is it to be diverted? Alerted? Permitted to interrupt myself? How helpful is it to my work, to my happiness, to my personal greater good?" When the wandering mind never arrives at a destination, lack of purpose and lack of fulfillment are the unwelcome results. Yes, it's hard to keep the wandering mind on the path of sustained focus, because seeking interruption is natural. Few, and certainly not I, will dispute that it requires great discipline and, most importantly, ongoing practice to stay on task.

As you have worked very hard in Part I of this book to convert unfocused behavior into positive action, now is not the time to backslide. It can be so easy to become sidetracked on the job, and the tougher the challenge, the more tempting almost any distraction can be. But you must keep focused on the goals you've established, the outcomes you've clearly defined, and your daily to-do list for getting you there or you will jeopardize your 100 Day Plan. And, speaking of to-do lists, create or find one! Use a dynamic to-do list, like the one below, that you will need to redo first thing every day to keep your focus sharp and your foot on the accelerator.

THINGS TO DO TODAY

Priority		Date _____ Completed
☐ 1.	_____	☐
☐ 2.	_____	☐
☐ 3.	_____	☐
☐ 4.	_____	☐
☐ 5.	_____	☐
☐ 6.	_____	☐
☐ 7.	_____	☐
☐ 8.	_____	☐
☐ 9.	_____	☐
☐ 10.	_____	☐
☐ 11.	_____	☐
☐ 12.	_____	☐
☐ 13.	_____	☐
☐ 14.	_____	☐
☐ 15.	_____	☐

If it ain't great, we don't do it;
if it ain't great, we don't show it!

Keeping your foot on the accelerator is all about one thing: discipline. A writer friend of mine, who was let go by his employer and then decided to become a freelancer (which he has been for twenty successful years now), explains it this way:

"A lot of creative people in my department were let go at the same time I was. Many of them decided to go out on their own too, but most of them didn't make it. It's a tough road and any little interruption—a text message from a friend, a news report about the Steelers going to the Super Bowl, or whatever—can be most welcome. OK, so I'll return that text message, spread the news about the Steelers, and take a little break, what's the difference?

"I'll tell you! The difference is that all these little breaks add up. You've got to stay focused on your objectives every minute of every working day, and that requires the discipline not to jump and return phone calls right away. It means turning off your smartphone, declining unnecessary meetings, and eliminating anything else from your daily to-do list that isn't relevant to reaching your target."

This good advice applies whether you happen to be a freelancer, a senior executive, or a factory floor supervisor.

Multitasking has had its fifteen minutes of fame. Today and tomorrow, it's about focus, focus, focus.

MEMO FROM SANDER

If you shudder when your teenager claims to be more productive doing his or her homework while listening to an iPod, texting friends, checking out Facebook or Twitter, or playing video games, it may be because the behavior reminds you of yourself at work. Sure you can get a lot of things done if you're a skilled juggler, but how many of those things are really being done well? Are you settling for too much "B" or even "C" work? Are you taking shortcuts that can come back to bite you simply to be the master of multitasking? Multitaskers may appear impressive; however, our research confirms my personal observations that their work typically falls well short of the mark.

5. Learn and Teach Those around You to Embrace Change

It's often said that the two things people fear most are public speaking and death, in that order. In my opinion though, change really heads the list. This is certainly true in the environment of work (see Chapter 1). Employees go to their workplace every day knowing that the coffee machine is securely in the same spot and the combination to the lavatory is 1-3-5. All is well and good in their world; a stable environment is what keeps their world happy. But then...

Word comes down the company has been acquired and a new boss will be coming in two weeks. And the common reaction is: "Oh my God, what's going to happen to me now?"

MEMO FROM SANDER

No book sums up the fear of change as succinctly as Spencer Johnson's runaway best seller *Who Moved My Cheese?* It is a parable of mice and humans dealing with change while living in a complex maze. But would change be nearly as frightening if we remembered another runaway best seller, *Curious George?* Curious George is never afraid to try something new. Does he get into lots of trouble along the way and make us laugh? Sure. But he also shows us how much fun it is to set out on an adventure and expand our horizons.

From the factory floor to the executive suite, people absolutely ABHOR change. And yet to succeed in today's expanding dynamic marketplace, employees in every capacity must learn to embrace and even welcome it. And if you haven't done so already, the time to begin is during the one hundred days of starting your new job or settling into your new promotion. Time waits for no man or woman. Resist change and you will be out of a job and maybe unemployed for a long time. Embrace change and you're on your way to a secure future.

Hanna Rosin's controversial best seller *The End of Men: And the Rise of Women* addresses this very subject head-on, insisting that because women are more adaptable to change, they have a huge edge over men in this dynamic environment. Not unexpectedly, her thoughts have created quite a stir. One of my favorite columnists, David Brooks of the *New York Times,* devoted an entire column to her idea entitled "Why Men Fail."

Brooks writes that men are coming up short—they earn only forty percent of the bachelor and master degrees issued by today's colleges and universities whereas women earn sixty percent of them. In my leadership class at Fordham University Graduate School of Business Administration, I see the same 40/60 gender split. Only a decade ago the split went the other way!

Brooks posits that what's turned the roles around is adaptability to change. Men are slower to accept change; women adapt faster to new paradigms. Brooks makes an analogy with immigrants. Some adapt and thrive in their new homeland; others never learn the new language and customs, remaining expats all their lives.

I have a different thought. Many women rise through the ranks because they possess the ability and resourcefulness to adjust better to fast-moving changes inherent in large organizations. Yet, not to my liking, what I have also observed is some women succumb to the misconception that, when they reach the pinnacle, they must act like the leadership patriarchs of old, and—forgetting what got them to the top to begin with—they start acting like command-and-control men.

This might explain the unexpected falls, after meteoric rises, that we often see with women in the business world. And, looking across the aisle at men, it might also explain why machismo-like work behavior hampers men on every level of the ladder. "Acting like a man" doesn't mean acting like a "macho" man. The workplace rule book has changed, and it pays to embrace change.

> **MEMO FROM SANDER**
>
> Younger workers today are gravitating away from employment by big companies to seek jobs at smaller, growing ones. They prefer the entrepreneurial atmosphere of those companies, where something new and exciting is happening every single day. In other words, they love change and expect to hold many different jobs over the course of their working lives rather than retiring in thirty or forty years from the same one. It's a different world out there and if you want to succeed in it, you'd better be able to pivot quickly and roll with the punches—or hope you're set to retire.

6. Leave Your Mark.

Building a proud legacy is, to my way of thinking, one of the most important objectives we can work on during our time on this earth. None of us wants to be thought of as average or inconsequential during our lives. On a personal level, we want to be thought of—and remembered—as kind and loving spouses, partners, parents, children, siblings, relatives, and friends. And on the professional level, don't we want a legacy that says we were the best we could be at our respective trades? Building that professional legacy begins with doing A-Plus work, starting your first day on the job and never stopping.

Legacy building also demands having a degree of paranoia—a trait I find is a good one to have at every level of employment. I don't mean the kind of paranoia that says to keep looking over your shoulder for that knife in the back or above your head for the axe to fall. I mean the kind of benign paranoia that keeps you asking yourself:

Am I constantly looking for new ideas and better ways to achieve greater outcomes?

Is this just an OK plan or a great one?

Am I seen at all times as the "doer"?

Do I read everything I can lay my hands on so that I always know what's going in my field concerning social networking, socioeconomics, research, marketing, sales, presentation skills, leadership, finance, or whatever?

The most effective leaders in business and virtually every other profession, who have accomplished great things in their respective fields, share the kind of paranoia that says: "I don't want anyone to be better or smarter than me. So that means I really, really have to work harder than anybody else to stay on top of my game."

Can you imagine the late Steve Jobs standing by and letting another company come up with a better, more versatile computer tablet or smartphone than Apple? No! I'm sure it's what kept him up at night. And he nourished his paranoia to prevent him from ever slipping to number two in ideas, marketing savvy—you name it—to anyone. He used it to build his legacy as the best ever at what he did.

You don't have to be a Steve Jobs, or even a CEO for that matter, to build a legacy of excellence in your workplace. No matter what position you are in—newly self-employed, the new boss, the new underling, or the brand-new hire at any level—you must create and nourish a leadership mindset in order to leave your mark. That's what this chapter—in fact, this whole book—is really about. You must WANT to build your legacy because that's what A-Plus performers do. If you're a writer of books, for example, you want them to be best sellers and not be sent to the bargain bin within six weeks. So best-sellerdom is what you always shoot for—even if you don't make it.

MEMO FROM SANDER

Good listening skills-fast disappearing yet so valuable to successful outcomes-are essential to developing a leadership mindset. This mindset means having high enough self-esteem to be willing to listen to those who work for, or with, you. You don't want "yes men" or "yes women." You don't want people who will always nod their heads in agreement to everything you say. You want pushback from people who are as smart as, or smarter than, you in areas where you are deficient. That's having a leadership mindset!

Nobody who hopes to keep moving forward into the next great chapter of their lives can afford to be average—not any longer. You must want to stand out and be the person who gets the calls from bosses, clients, and coworkers because they know you're the go-to guy or gal who gets the job done. You're the one who can keep your cool in a crisis. You're the one who reads all the time to keep on top of the latest trends in the field. You're the one who researches more deeply to connect the dots and come up with those big win-win ideas. You're the one who is willing to work harder than anybody else.

MEMO FROM SANDER

Pay attention and seek to understand emerging technologies, products, systems, and strategies. Be paranoid about getting your boss's and your colleagues' buy-in to your vision and execution. Be very paranoid about how you are connecting with clients and customers. Be paranoid that you're not being paranoid enough. Your future is at stake-and your legacy.

That's the mark you want to leave at whatever you do, wherever you work. It's the reason to hold your head up and know not only have you survived but, undeniably, you have thrived beyond your own expectations! So, when you look back at the traumatic event that brought you to this book, you can say of that career setback: "Look at me now. That really was the best thing that could ever have happened to me!"

Appendix

Selected References

Selected Job-Search Contacts

Throughout this book I have stressed the importance of reaching out to friends, confidants, mentors, former bosses, and coworkers for job leads and recruiter contacts. The following is a selected list of reputable outplacement companies and services as well as executive and niche recruiters nationwide that you might want to consider reaching out to on your own.

Outplacement Companies/Services

ACF North America

Directory of North American outplacement and career transition firms

http://www.acf-northamerica.com

704-849-2500

Allen and Associates

Career development and career marketing services

http://www.allenandassociates.com

866-953-8800

Executive Coaching Group

Executive coaching for individuals wanting to take their careers to the next level

http://www.executivecoachgroup.com

212-877-3400

Impact Group

Career transition, outplacement, and relocation support

http://www.impactgrouphr.com/home.aspx

info@impactgrouphr.com

314-453-9002

800-420-2420

Prositions, Inc

Tailored outplacement and transition services

http://prositions.com

877-244-8488

Quest Outplacement

Outplacement services for all types of downsized employees, including executive-level

http://www.questoutplacement.com

info@questoutplacement.com

888-430-2637

Staffing Industry Analysts

Research and analysis firm covering the contingent workforce. Information for decision-makers who supply and buy temporary staffing

http://www.staffingindustry.com

800-950-9496

The Dublin Group

Boutique staffing firm that specializes in temporary and direct hire placement of professionals

http://www.thedubingroup.com

800-851-5478

The Five O'clock Club

National outplacement, career development, and career coaching services

http://fiveoclockclub.com

hr@fiveoclockclub.com

212-286-4500

800-538-6645

Top Executive and Niche Recruiters

The firms below work in a variety of industry, functional, local, or specialty practices. Since recruiting and search demands change, we advise you to view the websites or contact the firms to research your specific needs.

Bench International
http://www.benchinternational.com
310-854-9900

DHR International
http://www.dhrinternational.com
312-782-1581

Egon Zehnder International
http://www.egonzehnder.com
212-519-6000

Heidrick & Struggles
http://www.heidrick.com
312-496-1200

IIC Partners
http://iicpartners.com
614-798-8500 ext. 125

Korn Ferry International
http://www.kornferry.com
310-552-1834

McBryde & Partners
http://www.mcbrydepartners.com
marnie@mcbrydepartners.com
212-752-9155

Ray & Berndtson
http://www.rayberndtson.com
candidate@ rayberndtson.com

Russell Reynolds
http://www.russellreynolds.com
hcamericas@russellreynolds.com
212-351-2000

Spencer Stuart
http://www.spencerstuart.com
312-822-0088

Additional Reading

Here are books I recommend to help deepen your understanding of what it takes to become—and remain—a valued employee and an A-Plus player in a highly competitive job market.

Flaum, Sander A. *Big Shoes: How Successful Leaders Grow into New Roles*. CreateSpace Independent Publishing Platform, 2009.

Roberts, Wess PhD. *Leadership Secrets of Attila the Hun*. Business Plus, 1990.

Schawbel, Dan. *Me 2.0: Build a Powerful Brand to Achieve Career Success*. Kaplan Publishing, 2009.

Morgenstern, Julie. *Never Check E-Mail in the Morning: And Other Unexpected Strategies for Making Your Work Life Work*. Touchstone, 2005.

Tracy, Brian. *Reinvention: How to Make the Rest of Your Life the Best of Your Life*. AMACOM, 2009.

Qualman, Erik. *Socialnomics: How Social Media Transforms the Way We Live and Do Business*. Wiley, 2012.

Porras, Jerry, Stewart Emery, and Mark Thompson. *Success Built To Last: Creating a Life That Matters*. Plume, 2007.

Flaum, Sander A., Jonathon A. Flaum, and Mechele Flaum. *The 100-Mile Walk: A Father and Son on a Quest to Find the Essence of Leadership*. Amacom, 2006.

Lafley, A.G. and Ram Charan. *The Game-Changer: How You Can Drive Revenue and Profit Growth with Innovation.* Crown Business, 2008.

Boynton, Andy, Bill Fischer, and William Bole. *The Idea Hunter: How to Find the Best Ideas and Make Them Happen.* Jossey-Bass, 2011.

Hamel, Gary. *What Matters Now: How to Win in a World of Relentless Change, Ferocious Competition, and Unstoppable Innovation.* Jossey-Bass, 2012.

Johnson, M.D., Spencer. *Who Moved My Cheese?: An Amazing Way to Deal with Change in Your Work and in Your Life.* G. P. Putnam's Sons, 1998.

Maxwell, John C. *Winning with People: Discover the People Principles That Work for You Every Time.* Thomas Nelson, 2007.

About The Author

Sander A. Flaum is the author of three books on career leadership and management. A renowned marketer, he is credited with the successful introduction of more than twenty leading pharmaceutical products. Sander is a featured speaker for many organizations, and he conducts workshops to stimulate creativity, spark innovation, improve sales productivity, and foster leadership. His seminars, Competitive War Games, Invitation to Innovate, and Test Flight are designed to help clients, facing marketing and brand leadership challenges, exceed their expectations.

Sander is a longtime champion of the Big Idea, which creates and infuses breakthrough thinking up and down the marketing chain, both in business and in his role as Adjunct Professor of Management Science and Executive-In-Residence at the Fordham University Graduate School of Business Administration, where he founded and chairs the Fordham University Leadership Forum. He was also the school's commencement speaker in 2001 and 2011.

Currently principal of Flaum Navigators, a marketing consulting company that provides consulting services in marketing, sales effectiveness, and leadership, Sander was chairman of Euro RSCG Life, a worldwide network of forty-three healthcare agencies. In addition, Sander presided over the growth of Robert A. Becker Inc. as it became the number two healthcare advertising agencies in the United States. *Med Ad News* named Becker "Agency of the Year" and Sander "Man of the Year" in 2002.

Earlier in his career, Sander worked for eighteen years at Lederle Laboratories (now Pfizer) where he became Marketing

Director and, during his tenure, honed his vision of the company he dreamed of finding as a client. The result became Flaum Navigators.

Sander has his BA from the Ohio State University and his MBA (magna cum laude) from Fairleigh Dickinson University. Prior to Fordham, Sander served on the faculty of New York University's Stern School of Business and is currently a member of the Conference Board's Mid-Level CEO Contingent. Sander is an active member of the American Management Association among other significant business, educational and professional organizations including Edge4Vets and the American Institute for Stuttering.

Along with his son Jonathon, Sander coauthored *The 100-Mile Walk: A Father and Son on a Quest to Find the Essence of Leadership* in 2006. He published *Big Shoes: How Successful Leaders Grow into New Roles* in 2009. Both books speak to the "rising stars of business" and focus on developing teams and cultivating a winning culture to move up in the organization. *The Best Thing That Could Ever Happen to You* provides a motivational how-to approach, and is for people facing change and disruption in their work lives.

In addition to his CEO, speaking, and writing activities, Sander has been widely interviewed on business and employment issues on CNBC and CNN and in *Business Week, Med Ad News, Pharmaceutical Executive*, the *New York Times*, and the *Wall Street Journal*. Sander has a weekly radio show, *The Leader's Edge* on WHDD FM and writes a monthly column for *Med Ad News* and *MWorld*, the online magazine of the American Management Association.

Sander is married to Mechele Flaum, his editor and best friend, and has two children, Pamela and Jonathon, and four grandchildren.

Index

CPSIA information can be obtained at www.ICGtesting.com
Printed in the USA
BVOW03s2330301013

335089BV00002B/3/P